LLEWELLYN'S
2005
WICCA
ALMANAC

Featuring

Elizabeth Barrette, Chandra Beal, Boudica, Dallas Jennifer Cobb, Ellen Dugan, Emely Flak, Karen Glasgow-Follett, Ruby Lavender, Paniteowl, Diana Rajchel, Flame Ravenhawk, Steven Repko, Cerridwen Iris Shea, Norman Shoaf, Tammy Sullivan, Dianne Sylvan, and S. Tifulcrum

Llewellyn's 2005 Wicca Almanac

ISBN 0-7387-0308-7. Copyright by Llewellyn Publications, St. Paul, Minnesota, USA. All rights reserved.

♻ Printed in the United States of America on recycled paper.

Editor/Designer: Michael Fallon

Cover Design: Gavin Dayton Duffy

Cover Images: © Digital Vision; © BrandX; © Photodisc

Interior Illustrations: Keri Smith 8, 12, 73, 77, 111, 114, 260; Claudine Hellmuth, 15, 19, 21, 83, 136, 139, 280, 283; Brian Raszka 24, 28, 58, 63, 144, 147, 273, 275, 277; Sean Qualls 33, 36, 93, 96, 152, 156; Tara Labus 41, 42, 45; Terry Miura 50, 103, 105, 241; Matt Kenyon 66, 118, 122, 229, 232, 265; Stefanie Augustine 118, 249, 253

Clip Art Illustrations: © PhotoDisc; © Brand X Pictures; © Digital Stock. Models are used for illustrative purposes only.

Special thanks to Amber Wolfe for the use of daily color correspondences. For more detailed information on this subject, please see *Personal Alchemy* by Amber Wolfe.

You can order Llewellyn annuals and books from *New Worlds,* Llewellyn's magazine catalog. To request a free copy of the catalog, call toll-free 1-877-NEWWRLD, or visit our website at http://subscriptions.llewellyn.com.

Moon sign and phase data computed by Astro Communications Services (ACS).

Llewellyn Worldwide
Dept. 0-7387-0308-7
P.O. Box 64383
St. Paul, MN 55164-0838

Llewellyn's 2005 Wicca Almanac

Table of Contents

Chapter One: Lifestyles of the Witch & Famous

Wiccan & Pagan fashions & lifestyles, media sightings, gossip & tidbits, & all things wicked & Witchy

Chapter Two: Witchcraft D.I.Y.

Do-it-yourself tips, how-tos, & empowering instructions for the very Wiccan & the extremely Witch-minded

Chapter Three: Sweep Me Away!

Tips & suggestions for Wiccans who wander through the wide & wondrous world

Almanac Section: Spring 2005 to Spring 2006

*The days & the nights, the Moon & the stars, the colors & the energies,
& all the latest Wiccan/Pagan news—the yearly almanac gives you everything
you need to get you through this heady astrological year*

Chapter Four: WWW

The Wicca Wide Web

Chapter Five: Over the Cauldron

*Up-to-date Wiccan opinions & rantings overheard
& spelled out just for you*

Chapter Six: Eye of Toad, Ear of Newt

A Wiccan/Pagan consumer guide

Introduction

Welcome, frazzled readers of the *2005 Wicca Almanac*. We acknowledge that you may be "frazzled" because we here at Llewellyn Central tend to keep a pretty realistic eye on the culture at large. Many in our mainstream culture prefer to think that everything is "fine," smiling endlessly and wishing others "a nice day," preoccupying themselves with lots of noise and flashing lights and wondering why they're more exhausted at the end of the week than at the beginning. We are not about that at all.

In fact, we're all about acknowledgement. It's the first step in seeking help to our frazzle-itis. As a result, the *Wicca Almanac* is a collection of the best and latest thinking about living the unfrazzled life, or at least how to deal with life. Check out page 90, for instance, for tips on blending your current hip Wicca practice with a bit of yoga. Or maybe you'll like the article on page 151, which has trips on how to travel across country in comfort and peace. All through this edition, along with yearly calendar and holiday information, you will find in-depth and opinionated articles on current fashions, on Pagan art and music, on Wiccans and Witches in the media, on travel, on using the web, on Pagan festivals, and so on—all written by innovative young thinkers and expert writers on these subjects. On the whole, the *Wicca Almanac* is geared to the do-it-yourself aesthetic, to young practitioners of the world's most ancient spiritual traditions who still fancy themselves independent thinkers, and to a frazzle-free lifestyle.

If, after you read this yearbook, you have some tips of your own you'd like to offer, please send them to us (at the address on page 2, or at annuals-submissions@llewellyn.com). If we like what you write, we'll publish it in the next edition of this book. And we hope you find some peace in your life in the meantime.

Lifestyles of the Witch & Famous

Wiccan & Pagan fashions & lifestyles, media sightings, gossip & tidbits, & all things wicked & Witchy

Our Familiar Friends:
Wiccans and Their Pets
by Chandra Beal

Witches have long been associated with animal companions, known as "familiars." In the past such familiars were spiritual beings who assisted in magic—sometimes appearing in physical bodies, and sometimes working unseen on other levels of existence. Some familiars represent the spirits of beloved pets that have passed on from the physical plane. Others work with us from the wild, or exist as animal totems, representing their unique qualities and guiding us on our daily path.

The concept of the "familiar," a spirit used by Witches, shamans, and magicians to enhance their magic, is old. The word

comes from the Latin *famulus,* meaning "attendant." A familiar is also sometimes known as a "fetch." Familiars are used to strengthen your magic, warn you of danger, guide you on inner or shamanic journeys, for healing, to adapt an animal's traits for shape-shifting, and to help us understand the connection between humans, animals, plants, and the universe.

The most popular kind is the animal familiar, but there are many other kinds of familiars—such as plants, elementals, deities, and the spirits of the dead. Animals are our connection to the divine. Myths abound that tell of a magical time and place in which there were no boundaries between humans and animals, a time of mingling between divine and human. Humans in these stories are at peace with animals, speaking the same language and communicating for the good of all.

Animals and Human Experience

Animals have always been part of the human experience, as evident from images painted and drawn on cave walls. Animals are mentioned in the creation stories and ancient prophecies of native tribes worldwide. Today, familiars most often appear as our modern companions, pets. Whether or not we share our magical workings with them and include them in rituals, animals offer us valuable lessons for living in the modern world and evoking magic.

The unconditional love of an animal is magic at its crest. Unfortunately, humans are not so great at loving unconditionally. This part of divinity has been all but lost to us over the millennia. Animals, however, can still tap into this font and can teach us much in the **Animals have always been part of human experience, as evident from images on cave walls.** process. Animals can climb into our very souls, soothing and alerting us when necessary, and protecting us and guiding us. Magic still flows with and through the animals of this planet as it has from the beginning.

For example, animals can feel spirits. That is, pets are often observed responding to sights, smells, and sounds beyond the comprehension of our human senses. They feel impending earthquakes, know when their humans are coming home, and tune into worlds inaccessible to us. Many people dismiss animals as "dumb" because they communicate in ways different from ours, but animals actually possess skills long lost to most of us.

The souls of pets and humans usually are linked together through lifetimes of experience with each other. In many instances, our pets may have spent other incarnations with us in past lifetimes, returning to us to continue unfinished work. Sometimes they may reincarnate more than once with us in the same lifetime, as their life span is much shorter than ours.

The animal world still has much to teach us, if only we can be open to it. Some animals are expert at survival and adaptation. Some animals are great nurturers and protectors. Some have great fertility and creative energy, and others possess gentleness, strength, loyalty, courage, or playfulness. The animal world shows us the innate potential of life—our inner magic and power.

The Forms of Familiars

Most familiars today take a physical form. Our pets and companion animals are the most obvious potential magical familiars in our lives. The black cat is probably the most popular stereotype of a familiar, but dogs, rabbits, and many other domestic creatures are popular, and each has its own particular magic to share. Many other small creatures, such as crows, rats, and toads, to name a few, have also been associated with Witches.

Because of their power, familiars, like their Witchy companions, were mistrusted and misunderstood. During the Dark Ages, it was thought that every Witch possessed familiars or imps disguised as household pets, and it was thought these creatures were given to Witches by the devil. It was believed that familiars could convey messages over long distances, could frighten the horses and livestock of one's enemies, and could spy on people and gather intelligence. If a woman was suspected to be a Witch and imprisoned, her persecutors would observe her in her cell and if even a small insect visited, it was assumed to be a messenger from the devil. Many innocent lives were taken thanks to this belief.

Besides providing us with the sheer pleasure of their company, familiars can join us during rituals and spell work. They may weave in and out of a sacred circle, acting as official greeter. They may help raise vibrational energy with their presence, and can keep practitioners grounded and protected from malevolent beings. Some pets have connections to deities associated with their kind (for instance, rabbits and Ostara, or dogs and Artemis), and can tap into the power of their associated figures. Keep in mind, however, that while some domestic animals love participating in rituals, others prefer to find a quiet corner to curl up and take a nap.

A question you may ask is, how do you know you are working with a familiar as opposed to just sharing space with a pet? If an animal is more than it appears, more than anything you will know it intuitively. You can hear them if you keep our hearts and minds open. Anyone with a close bond to their pet seems to know exactly what the pets needs. You will develop a psychic-kinetic bond, and you will suddenly realize that unspoken feelings exist between the two of you. Animals' psychic senses are highly developed because their minds aren't cluttered with all the junk and chattering that runs through our minds on any given day. You may find too that your animal often appears to you in dreams or visions, or tries to present you with a message. They might lead you into synchronicities, helping you meet the right people on the path or putting you in the right place at the right time.

Since Wiccans believe in the sanctity of all life, familiars should be held in respect as individual spirits, part of the great wheel of life. Respect is important to a familiar. They come to you to guide and help you, and to give you messages. These are all important. Honor your pets and show respect by thanking them, giving them a treat or a special toy, or leaving a token of some kind on your altar to your animal's totem spirit.

If you don't have pets for whatever reason, you can still attract a familiar of the astral kind. All you need to do is meditate on a chosen familiar and call for it—though this does not mean the familiar will come to attend you just because you call. Familiars have free will and will come if they want to and feel they have something necessary for you. Sometimes they come for a short period and leave when their work is done. Some may choose us even if we don't call them.

The key to attracting a familiar is patience and listening with all your senses. To call upon a familiar you must be acquainted with the particular qualities of each one. Spend some time reading about any animal you feel drawn to, and think about which of their qualities you respect and want to learn from. Familiars may come to you through a vision, meditation, or dream. Sometimes a familiar's messages will be subtle, so watch carefully.

intuition

The connection between humans and pets can be deeply intense. Most pets want nothing more than to bring their owner unconditional love, caring, guidance, and a feeling of protection. Humans find pets very comforting because of all these qualities. Pets also absorb our negative feelings. If we're feeling depressed, sad, fearful, or angry, our pets pick up on our feelings and help us deal with them on an instinctual level.

When we walk through the door after a hard day, our pets immediately know how we are feeling and they greet us accordingly— maybe with a few extra kisses or wags of the tail or maybe with calm patience as they wait for us to feel better again. Other animal familiars provide us with healing to enrich our magical work, bringing us back in contact with the divine spark that flows through all of us.

Whether you're living with a loyal companion animal who gives you simple friendship and protection, or working with a magical deity in a furry body, pets are an integral part of our lives and can offer us much wisdom in life.

Superior Sabbat Foods

by Steven Repko

Our spirits change with the seasons as we mark each spoke of the wheel of the year with a sabbat celebration. At these special times, Pagans gather together in an atmosphere of love, sharing, and fellowship to observe the time of the season and to take joy in our relationships with the gods and each other. We do this with song, we do it with ritual, and of course, we do it with food.

The sabbat feasts of today draw inspiration from ancient traditions. These are a secret of life passed along in regional customs, religious commemorations, and ethnic revels. It is fitting that at these special times of the year we recognize that

13

food was not just a part of the celebration, but it was actually the prize celebrated by the holiday.

Most of us can think back to childhood memories of seasonal holidays in our homes. These memories likely involve a collage of heavenly sights and smells—cookies and candies, roasts and soups, fruits, pies, cakes, creams, puddings, and spices. No matter what our upbringing, ethnic or religious background, all of us are encoded with an understanding of holiday magic. Looking back into history, we can see that life long included the threat of possible starvation during times of famine. We need to remember that the ancients celebrated a good harvest and hunt through their holiday blessings.

It is through the holidays that we first learn to share as a community our love of life.

What the Holiday Foods Teach Us

It was through the holidays that we first learned to share as a community our love of life. We experience love by association when we recall the recipes we sampled and passed down through our families: grandma's chicken paprikash, Aunt Mary's egg noodles in broth, and Aunt Bertie's steak in the oven. These auspicious culinary events represent an individual labor of love, and they help ingrain in us a sense of seasonal rejoicing. It is by sharing these special holiday delights that we truly come together in love and timeless celebration.

When it comes to food, the old ways are usually best—perhaps because there was always so little to entertain us, in comparison with today, that food was a more central focus in the past. People spent much time in the kitchen. Many times the meal was prepared only after the ingredients themselves were produced in the same pantry. Many of my favorite foods have to marinate for days, cook for hours, or require more than one preparation step. Yes, good food can be intimidating, but it is worth it—especially during the holidays.

of chopped tarragon in
butter. When half coo

Through the years I have also learned a few things I don't like about the old ways. For instance, chocolate pudding out of the box is easier to make, and I can't tell the difference between that and scratch-made pudding. I like more sugar in my root beer than they did back in the old days. When experimenting your way through old recipes, you may often have to adjust sugar and spice to suit your modern tastes. Even in my pizza dough there is three times more sugar than called for.

What I do like is simple. People once were literally closer to the soil, and because of this they had a closer relationship with what the soil provided. If you wanted basil, for instance, you grew basil.

Always know, therefore, the quality of the ingredients you are using—it is important. When you look at a piece of meat you should have a good idea if it's good or bad, tough or soft. Check to be sure fruits and vegetables are ripe. And so on. We have been taught by the modern food providers that we can get strawberries and tomatoes and so on all year long, but we also forget that these foods are supposed to have flavor.

If you are lucky enough to still have grandparents, go shopping with them. Observe and learn from them—they know much more about food quality than the rest of us who grew up in the era of packaged food. Learn their lore as well. I may look ridiculous whispering to the pears and onions (as per my grandmother's method), but I refuse to buy produce that is of lower quality than I expect. One has a better chance making a silk purse of a sow's ear than making a sweet sauce of bad produce.

Sabbat Food Celebrations

In my coven, we thank the gods daily for the opportunity to celebrate every sabbat just talking and eating. Our holidays revolve around the menus. I've learned, however, that it's always a good idea to set up seasonal guidelines for food. These can be practical—concerning keeping food cool for outdoor events and avoiding using mayonnaise if it will be warm; or aesthetic—planning what will go with roast beef and turkey. Take some time and talk about what people are bringing, how the dishes will be served, and suggest complimentary foods.

Every year at Yule, for instance, we have a large all-night festival that ends in a dawn ritual on the beach. We do not need to worry about what the other attendees will bring because our plan follows the full meal model. That is, as per Sunday dinners of my youth, everyone plans to bring a main meal such as roast turkey, or a side dish such as mashed potatoes or baked macaroni and cheese, or a cake for dessert. However many people we think will attend, we make just enough to feed them. When everyone else brings food using the same model, we all eat very well.

Some foods are always a major hit. Deviled eggs are probably number one, but stuffed mushrooms are also a favorite at our gatherings. Fresh bread sets a mood of sharing, and the recipes collected below usually serve us very well. Although not by any stretch a major project, fresh bread is impressive both in its dining satisfaction and in its representation of hospitality. The idea is that someone took the time to shape this loaf by hand, so they must have really cared. Also, bread is magical because it is very easily torn and passed from person to person— like a piece of good news or a wish for the future.

There are few foods more recognizable to the senses than a browning crust on a hearty loaf.

Our Daily Bread

2 tsps. dry yeast

4 cups flour

1 tsp. salt

2 Tbls. sugar

3 Tbls. oil

1½ cups water

To make this recipe, in a bowl mix all ingredients with a wooden spoon for ten minutes, then let it set for thirty minutes. Beat down the dough, knead it for twenty minutes, and let it sit for an hour. Flour and shape the dough into a long loaf, leave in a warm place for an hour, then pop it into a 400°F oven for twelve minutes or until nice and brown. A bread machine or large mixer can make this a lot less work.

This bread is truly alive with the spirits of the air (yeast) and earth (wheat). It represents the sacrifice of the fields and is related in mythology as one of the gifts of divine providence. I have taken this bread dough and shaped it into the Sun shape for a Lammas feast. I have also shared it on Hallowmas Eve, and, with a half-cup of cocoa and a few tablespoons more sugar, I have served a version of this bread at Yule.

Is it any wonder that almost every religion contains a cele-bratory ceremony of the breaking and sharing of bread? Perhaps man doesn't live by bread alone, but the humble loaf represents the toil of man, the grace of the gods, and what can be accomplished through the cooperation of both in harmony.

A Magical Sabbat Meal

Got a cauldron and a few hours? Make a magical sabbat meal to remember.

Real Hungarian Goulash

¼ cup oil

2 lbs. beef or veal

1 lb. mushrooms, sliced

1 large onion, sliced

6 carrots, sliced

5 celery stalks, broken in half

1 Tbl. salt, or less to taste

5 potatoes, cut into cubes or quarters

1 pinch saffron

In a twelve-inch pot over high heat combine the oil, meat, mushrooms, and onion. Cook until the meat is browned.

Add the carrots, celery, salt, and saffron. Cover the mixture with water, and bring the pot to a boil. Reduce heat to medium-low, and cook covered for two hours, stirring occasionally and checking that the water doesn't boil out.

Remove the celery and purée it in a food processor. Return the puree to the pot, and add the potatoes. Bring the soup to a boil, and cook at a medium heat covered for thirty minutes, or until the potatoes are soft.

Although I do not, you can add some optional sour cream at the end. Serve this soup with fresh bread, of course.

This recipe is a hit at fire circles when brought in a large commercial pot. Just precook the soup and reheat it on the fire. This recipe serves five to eight people.

The magical realm is not without beverage options, so there's no need to worry. That is, through the wheel of the year we can find or prepare a number of unique and magical seasonal drinks to toast the holiday with.

There are many fruit juices available now that were once thought rare and exotic. Your local supermarket or gourmet shop is a treasure trove of beverages. There is of course the humble grape juice, in both red and white, apple juice, cranberry juice, and citrus juices of every variety.

The pomegranate comes with underworld mythology, and passion fruit can add an exotic touch to the festivities. The Bible spoke of the tree of life, and some scholars have deduced that the quince is the tree that best matches the description. The juice of the pear is a rare and wonderful drink, and peach nectar is akin to the "nectar of the gods." Although harder to come by, rose water from the Middle East can provide a unparalleled sensory experience, as your brain tries to cope with the taste of something that is more commonly smelled.

On the alcoholic side, there are May wines and bock beers for Beltane, along with mead and Octoberfest specialties for Samhain. I have used blackberry wine on Candlemas and elderberry wine on a Midsummer's night. Wassail mixes can make this traditional favorite suitable for Yule. Good old eggnog is a favorite for a night of Yule caroling and fire gazing. There are wines and beers flavored with everything from blueberries to watermelons, and a host of liquors and cordials to please even the pickiest deity. A little lore and a lot of imagination can go a long way.

As wonderful as any sabbat meal can be, the best is always saved for last. Desserts are a form of magic all their own. Cakes and pies, fruit with chocolate, pudding, mousse, pastries, and ice cream—who doesn't love a little dessert?

Sabbat food should always reflect the spirit of the holiday, and desserts should delight the eye as well as the palate. One of my favorite desserts ever was when we roasted marshmallows over the candle of a jack-o-lantern

When it comes to food, the old ways are best—perhaps because in the past there was so little to entertain us that food was a more central focus.

on Hallowmas Eve. My own imagination has given birth to pineapples with mocha mousse and the amazing recipe below, suitable for Candlemas Eve.

Brigit's Blackberry Forest Cheesecake

4 Tbls. butter, melted

1 cup graham cracker crumbs

⅝ cup sugar

4 pkg. (8 oz. each) cream cheese, softened

1 tsp. vanilla extract

4 eggs

12 oz. real semisweet chocolate chips, melted

1 can blackberry pie filling

Whipped cream or non-dairy topping

In a bowl, combine the butter and graham cracker crumbs with three tablespoons sugar, and mix until moist. Press the mixture into the bottom of a nine-inch springform pan, and bake the whole at 325°F for ten minutes.

Mix the cream cheese and vanilla extract with the remaining half-cup of sugar with an electric mixer on medium speed until the mixture is well blended. Add one egg at a time and mix at low speed until blended.

Add and blend in the melted chocolate. Bake the cake at 325°F for 55 minutes to one hour, or until center is almost set.

When the cake is finished cooking, run a knife around the rim of the pan to loosen the cake.

Cool the cake fully before removing the rim of the springform pan. Refrigerate the cake for four hours or overnight.

Garnish the center with blackberry pie filling and the outside edge with fresh whipped cream or non-dairy topping.

You may want to make two of these beauties.

Don't forget the coffee!

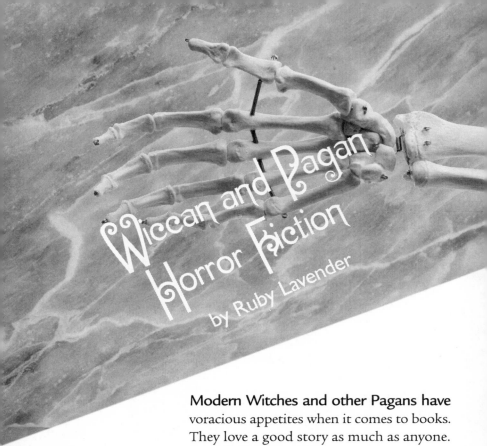

Wiccan and Pagan Horror Fiction
by Ruby Lavender

Modern Witches and other Pagans have voracious appetites when it comes to books. They love a good story as much as anyone.

While the majority of fiction with Pagan elements or themes tends to be of the fantasy, historical romance, or swords-and-sorcery variety, there are a growing number of novels which fall into the realm of something slightly darker: horror fiction, thriller, or good old-fashioned juicy mystery.

In this article I will mention a few of my favorite such books in the hope that they whet the appetites of those looking to expand their curl-up-and-read pleasure.

My one criterion for including books in this article is that they actually scared me—whether only slightly or in ways that made me want to keep my lights on all night. Other than that, no particular kind of story took precedence over any other.

The Wiccan Reading Audience

Before I begin, one thing I want to mention is that there are not very many books written with a "Wiccan" audience in mind. So for the most part the books I refer to will be of interest to those involved with witchcraft or other Pagan practices, and not Wicca specifically. There are many, many works of literature with occult themes and plots, and many horror writers work in the milieu of magic and mysticism. I have omitted them because most readers already associate Clive Barker, Stephen King, and H. P. Lovecraft with horror—my interest for this article was in identifying some novels with Pagan themes that might not necessarily fit neatly into the horror genre.

> Everyone knows a true Witch must understand the full continuum of magical power—from light to dark—in order to comprehend its function and potential.

The second thing I need to say up front is that a horror novel dealing with Paganism and witchcraft is not very likely to portray the Pagan characters as being life-affirming, working for the good of all, or involved with magic only for benevolent purposes or for their own positive self-transformation. These are stories, and as such they appeal to the imagination—so there is plenty of evil, black magic, spells intended to wreak havoc and cause harm, and healthy dashes of murder and mayhem throughout. So if you only want to read books where Witches are the good guys, you may want to do your own research and skip these books. Besides, everyone knows a true Witch must understand the full continuum of magical power—from light to dark—in order to comprehend its function and potential.

BRIANRASZKA.COM

The Scary Book List

The titles listed below are presented in no particular order, but I will be focusing on books and authors I have actually read and enjoyed. They range in dates of publication from the 1970s to the present, and all of these books are still in print or easily available online.

Cat Magic by Whitley Streiber (St. Martin's Press, 1986). This is a fun novel by an author we usually associate with books on fictionalized "real-life" UFO encounters. In this novel, a young female character, Amanda, goes to live in a Pagan homesteading community remarkably like the one portrayed in the film *The Wicker Man*, except that this takes place in the United States, and the characters are all fairly normal. Still, they're Pagans trying to run a self-sustaining village. Most of what occurs here is implausible, but the writing is rich with detail and atmosphere, and it can be quite spooky at times.

Lammas Night by Katherine Kurtz (Ballantine Books, 1983). This one is interesting because it's based on real life. Maybe some of you have heard that a group of Witches, many of them elderly, lived together in southern England in the 1930s to work magic during World War II to prevent Hitler from invading England. The working was successful, but several of the coven lost their lives. It's probably never going to be possible to prove that this actually happened, but it does make a fascinating tale. This intelligent and suspenseful novel tells the whole story in rather absorbing detail.

The Witches of Eastwick by John Updike (Knopf, 1984). Yes, John Updike, author of dozens of novels about small-town New Englanders, is also a horror author. Well, maybe not exactly a horror author, but this excellent novel does contain some truly frightening elements. First, I must say this is nothing at all like the film version. Three Witches who are divorced and unhappy become excited when an odd stranger comes to their sleepy Rhode Island town. Their ensuing behavior is shocking—

competitive, dishonest, vicious—and they use magic to accomplish some morally questionable ends. No wonder Margot Adler dissed this one. Still, Updike is such a masterful storyteller and has such a rich, intricate way of writing, you won't be able to put this down.

Neverwhere by Neil Gaiman (Avon, 1998). An inventive and rather dark story of heroes and villains set in London's underground. It details what happens when a very ordinary guy gets suddenly pulled into a world that lies just beneath everyone's noticing. It is interesting in how it explores how we all might react if we spent a few days among society's invisible members—the poor and the homeless. The story is funny, charming, gorgeously written, and apt to make you look over your shoulder more than once.

American Gods by Neil Gaiman (HarperTorch, 2002). Many Pagans are familiar with Gaiman for his Sandman series of graphic novels. He is a prolific and immensely talented author with a wily grasp of mythology and fairy tales. He also knows how to bring the deepest darkness out of his characters. In this novel, a quiet but capable man who is released from prison finds himself working for an avatar who is trying to bring about a full-scale battle of the gods that might possibly end the world as we know it. People and gods alike do some not-so-nice things in this novel—be prepared to laugh out loud and also to be creeped out quite a bit.

The Wicker Man by Robin Hardy (Random House, 1978). Yes, this is a novelized version of the Pagan classic tale. And it is very well written and suspenseful, too. Some think it a satire of the highest order that a Pagan enclave on a remote Scottish island in the 1970s would want to lure a virginal policeman to make him a human sacrifice to their gods. Others might find this very frightening. It's a great read, either way.

Waking the Moon by Elizabeth Hand (Eos, 1996). Hand's style is poetic and visual. This story is unusual and sometimes hard to swallow, but it blends fantasy, horror, and contemporary thriller genres seamlessly. Three young characters dabble in dangerous magic and try to move on with their lives after tragedy strikes. The book looks at them twenty years later as one of them prepares to finish what she started long ago. Set on a fictional college campus, and with characters able to travel through time, this book will be appealing to anyone who has always suspected magic and mystery lie hidden in the ivory towers of academia. But there are also plenty of erotic and other spooky happenings for everyone else!

Children of the Night by Mercedes Lackey (Tor Books, 1994). This is one of those Diana Tregarde mysteries. A practicing Witch and a team of vampires band together to fight evil in a fantastical story of rock bands and Pagan subcultures. It is a well-written story that has actual Wiccan characters. Lackey's Tregarde is a wonderful creation: powerful and smart, but with the Wiccan way of seeing one's flaws in stark relief. Sometimes she realizes just a bit too late that she has gone too far.

Wicked by Gregory Maguire (HarperCollins, 2002). A wildly inventive and wickedly funny story that is familiar and yet completely new. Maguire tells the story of the Wizard of Oz, or more precisely, the Wicked Witch of the West, from the Witch's point of view. This has recently been made into an award-winning Broadway musical, but don't let that stop you from reading it. Maguire crafts a story that is profoundly moving and beautifully written, and rather scary at times.

Practical Magic by Alice Hoffman (Berkley, 1998). The film version made this story seem somewhat more lightweight than the novel, which is very subtle and brimming with emotion. Two sisters from an unconventional upbringing struggle to find love on their own terms. The "W" word is barely mentioned but we all get it. Along the way there is accidental death, attempted murder, loneliness, grief, and adolescent angst. Hoffman's evocative style is perfect for describing the natural world and all that it invokes in the characters.

Mythago Wood by Robert Holdstock (Avon Books, 1984). This is the story of a family that lives at the edge of an old English forest where reality is constantly shifting, perhaps due to the research writings of the family patriarch. A man struggles to help his delusional brother while being drawn deeper and deeper into a mystical vortex in the forest primeval. Holdstock's descriptions of ancient myth and legend are compellingly readable, and for those interested in psychology the story's central father-son struggle is far more entertaining to read than Robert Bly or Joseph Campbell.

Harvest Home by Thomas Tryon (Harvest Home, 1974). This novel was made into a TV miniseries starring Bette Davis in the early 1980s, and it has actually provided the basis for a number of existing ritual cycles performed by modern Pagans. A couple from Manhattan move with their teenage daughter to a bucolic New England village, and find that the "old ways" kept by the villagers, while charming, just might be a bit barbaric as well. It includes some wonderfully evocative language describing the activities of a modern fertility cult and the Earth Mother they worship.

Dreams Underfoot by Charles de Lint (Tor, 1994). This collection of stories is sometimes warm and funny, and sometimes rather frightening. The author frequently sets his stories and novels in the fictional Canadian city of Newford, an ordinary kind of place where quite a few extraordinary characters live. De Lint's work is usually described as "urban fantasy," full of Celtic lore and contemporary fairy creatures, but there is a decidedly modernistic dark edge to it as well. These stories are often linked to one another by the characters they have in common, which makes reading them somewhat akin to reading an episodic novel.

All Acts of Love and Pleasure: Gay and Lesbian Wiccans

by Elizabeth Barrette

Regardless of their sexual orientation, people feel a need to connect with the divine. In some religions, heterosexuality is considered the only valid path. In others, people of alternative sexuality are considered closer to divinity or stronger in magic. Wicca takes a middle road between these extremes. Over the years it has developed many branches, some of which especially appeal to gays and lesbians.

Tolerance

The title of this article comes from the famous Wiccan liturgy "The Charge of the Goddess." In part it says, "Let My worship be in the heart that rejoices, for behold—all acts of love and pleasure are My rituals."

Wicca thus teaches the ideals of sexual freedom and tolerance for diverse practices. The rule concerns not so much what Witches do or who they do it with, but how—as long as it's in a spirit of "love and pleasure." Furthermore, Wicca considers sexuality a sacred practice, a "ritual." It is not unholy, shameful, dirty, sinful, or otherwise denigrated as in some other religions.

Gay and lesbian people still face much discrimination in their everyday lives. They may lose their jobs, homes, custody of children—the same threats that Pagans face. Many mainstream churches do not welcome homosexual members. So when they "come out of the closet" by declaring themselves gay or lesbian, they often lose their spiritual community.

Paganism at large, and Wicca more specifically, tends to take a more tolerant stance. Many Wiccan circles and festivals gladly welcome gays and lesbians. They rarely prohibit homosexual members from serving as priest or priestess or in other important roles. Some also acknowledge homo-affectionate qualities in deities they may invoke. Thus, queer folks often feel more at home in a Pagan faith than in their childhood faith.

Gay and Lesbian Traditions

Within Paganism in general, and Wicca in particular, there lie some paths that are especially known for their homosexual tendencies. While not all gay and lesbian Pagans choose these traditions, and not all followers of these are necessarily homosexual, these paths merit special coverage here.

Dianic Wicca takes a strong feminine focus. It is the heart of feminist Paganism. Dianic covens customarily consist of only women, although in recent years, a few have accepted male members. They often practice monotheism, worshipping the Goddess alone. Those who include the God at all do so only in a role subordinate to the Goddess, such as her son or consort. Such covens tend to be egalitarian rather than hierarchical, and may include political activism among their goals. More recently, some practitioners have used "Artemesian Wicca" to distinguish the all-female, Goddess-only branch from those including men and Gods in subordinate roles. These qualities have made Dianic Wicca and its offshoots very attractive to lesbians, who have influenced the evolution of this tradition.

Feri Wicca (also spelled Faerie or Faery) is an ecstatic path which draws a lot of its material from Celtic lore. Practitioners often celebrate the masculine aspects of divinity. This is a high-energy path of self-exploration that includes some sex magic. It's especially known for its wild,

Wicca teaches the ideals of sexual freedom and tolerance for diverse practices— as long as it's in a spirit of "love and pleasure."

"fey" flavor, and a concurrent tendency to pry the frame from consensus reality and bend everything into interesting new shapes. Unlike most Pagan paths, Feri is not a fertility religion. The lower emphasis on male/female dynamics has opened the doors for male/male and other combinations. Also twined into this complex field are the Radical Faeries, a branch of political and spiritual activism arising out of the gay community and developing in a generally Pagan direction. Many gay men feel drawn to these practices.

Gay and Lesbian Deities

Around the world, people tell myths about gods and goddesses who had homosexual or bisexual affairs. Most pantheons include at least one same-sex pairing or a deity in charge of homoerotic relationships. These deities offer special support to gay and lesbian Wiccans who may wish to worship a god or goddess of congruent orientation. Here is a brief introduction to some of the more interesting examples.

Aphrodite Urania (Greek) reveals a lesser-known aspect of the popular love goddess. Aphrodite Urania is sometimes referred to as the Bearded Love Goddess. She appears as a masculine woman, wise in celestial matters. Hers is a fierce love with an intellectual component. Her color is the deep purple of evening skies and her stone is amethyst. Gay, lesbian, and other queer folk often favor this aspect.

Artemis/Diana (Greek/Roman) may be the most famous lesbian goddess. Famed for her independence, she lives in the woods with a band of nymphs. This ferocious huntress tends to kill men who foolishly spy on her or who interrupt her rites. She turns them into deer or bears for her hounds to tear apart. Myths and poems speak of her female lovers, especially Callisto. She also inspired the Dianic tradition, favored by many lesbian Wiccans.

Bassareus (Greek) is the effeminate aspect of Dionysus. This god of wine and ecstasy dresses as a woman, making love with Adonis and Achilles among many others. Men are excluded from many of his rites, and he adores independent women such as lesbians. He can also put men in touch with their feminine sides.

Chin (Mayan) brought union across the intricate class structure of his society. This dwarfish god caused young noblemen to fall in love with farm boys and other youths of the lower classes. These couples sometimes were wed in marriages fully

33

recognized by Mayan law. Chin makes an ideal patron for activists interested in legalizing homosexual marriages today.

Erzulie (Afro-Caribbean) can possess either men or women, and like the other loas, she has many aspects. Most often she appears as a heterosexual woman, but if her spirit fills a male worshipper she may send him after other men! Because of her devotion to all things sensual and beautiful, many gay men worship her. However, in her aspect Erzulie Taureau she manifests in a more Amazonian or lesbian mode.

Ganesha (Hindu) has the head of an elephant and the body of a rather plush man, and sometimes he even he has breasts. Known as the "remover of obstacles," he is beloved of homosexuals who find life full of trials. Ganesha is also the patron of anal sex. This endears him to gay men especially, and to some lesbians as well.

Inanna (Sumerian) has a husband, Dumuzi, and a devoted handmaiden, Ninshubur. This fertility goddess also holds sway over all matters of sex and gender. She can reputedly transform male to female, masculine to feminine. Her temples house diverse clergy, including men as priestesses and women as priests. Inanna especially appeals to effeminate gays and masculine lesbians.

Kuan Yin (Buddhist) represents compassion and serenity. This Bodhisattva protects women and children, forestalling her own divinity until all of humanity reaches enlightenment. Her followers renounce heterosexual marriage. Instead they may join societies like the Golden Orchid Association that combine spirituality, feminism, and lesbianism.

Loki (Norse) usually appears as a man, but this tricky shapeshifter can also appear as a woman or as an animal of either sex. His relationship with Odin sounds very lovely in many of the myths, though they are most often referred to as "blood brothers."

Shiva (Hindu) dances creation and destruction. His symbols include many normally attributed to goddesses: the crescent moon, snake, and various flowers. When he and the goddess Parvati joined into a hermaphroditic deity, Ardhanarishvara was born. Shiva is a patron of masturbation and homosexuality. Butch/femme couples may keep a Shiva-Lingam on their altar.

Xochiquetzal (Aztec) rules the underworld. Her emblems include marigolds, skulls, and spiders. She oversees crafts such as weaving and silversmithing. Her special interest is non-procreative sex: oral, anal, homosexual, anything done just for the fun of it. She attracts both gay and lesbian followers.

Zeus (Greek) has little in the way of sexual limits. He chases pretty young women and pretty young men with equal enthusiasm. In particular, in the most famous of his homoerotic affairs, the cupbearer Ganymede caught his eye. Nevertheless, Zeus remains a strong father figure, useful for gay parents.

Polarity and Magic

In most Wiccan traditions, practitioners worship the Goddess and the God together, often represented by a High Priestess and a High Priest respectively. The symbolism and structure of the ritual activity tends to reflect this duality. The emphasis falls on fertility and therefore on heterosexual imagery. For example, the High Priest may lower an athame into the chalice held by the High Priestess, thus symbolizing sexual union.

To gay and lesbian Wiccans, this can seem irrelevant, unfulfilling, or downright aggravating. People often prefer their religion to reflect their personal experience to some degree. Just as they appreciate having a deity similar to themselves, they like to see congruent ritual motifs too. So practitioners modify existing rites or invent new ones to meet these needs.

In a gay coven, the men may invoke two gods. In a lesbian coven, the women may invoke two goddesses. Variations on the chalice-and-blade maneuver are particularly charming. Gay men may each hold a blade, staff, or other masculine artifact and cross them. Goddess-worshipping men may, alternatively, both insert their athames into a chalice (representing the Goddess) on

the altar. Lesbians often pour the ritual wine back and forth from one chalice to the other. Sometimes one woman holds a chalice of wine and the other a chalice of milk, which they then pour into a cauldron or onto the ground. All of these embody the union of same-sex energies. This really intensifies the single power celebrated in such rites.

One particularly interesting dynamic is the butch/femme pairing; that is, a couple with two women, one with a masculine spirit (the butch) and one intensely feminine (the femme). They may or may not identify as lesbians. Some of them keep the chalice-and-blade custom, with the butch taking the masculine role and lowering the athame into the femme's chalice. Others prefer different symbolism. Gaining popularity is the Shiva-Lingam, a phallic rock nestled in a yoni-like stand. The Shiva represents the "stone cock" with which a butch makes love to a femme, and the Lingam represents the femme's *yoni*. So there is a strong gender polarity in this pairing, even though both partners are biologically female.

Gay men have served as cross-dressing or homosexual priests in many historic religions. Less often, women have served in similar roles. Today some are recreating these traditions. A gay Wiccan may

Around the world, people tell myths about gods and goddesses who had homosexual or bisexual affairs.

then dress as a woman and invoke the Goddess; a lesbian may dress as a man and invoke the God. Other times, a practitioner may cultivate a deliberately androgynous appearance, especially when invoking a trickster or shapeshifting deity. When we step outside the ordinary boundaries, these "liminal" states create magical energy and tremendous power.

Of all ceremonies, the issue of sexuality stands out most in handfastings. A recent book, *Handfasting and Wedding Rituals* by Raven Kaldera and Tannin Schwartzstein (Llewellyn, 2003), explores this territory in great depth and sensitivity. There is a handfasting for two gay men, and one for two lesbians. There is another for a butch/femme couple, which adapts heterosexual imagery. Two more rituals, magnificent in theatrics, creatively employ queer myth to offer a "Shapeshifter's Handfasting" and "The Rite of Aphrodite Urania" for those whose sex/gender does not fit neatly under any one label. In addition to addressing the needs of gay and lesbian couples, these ceremonies also offer ways in which homosexual clergy can manifest their full potential as officiants.

Conclusions

As humans, we have a male or female body. We may fall in love with a partner of the same or opposite polarity. Yet spirit is not limited by corporeal delineations of sex and gender. Each soul has masculine and feminine attributes—a deity we think of as "Goddess" has a masculine side, and one we think of as "God" has a feminine side. Wicca reminds us that magic and spirituality span the sex and gender spectrum.

Gay and lesbian Wiccans are, essentially, the same as heterosexual Wiccans. Their needs and desires are but variations on a theme. They may choose to practice as solitaries, in a homosexual coven, or in a mixed coven. In any case, they should be welcomed and appreciated for their particular gifts. The charge makes it crystal clear how the Goddess views sexuality—remember: "All acts of love and pleasure are My rituals."

Pagan Erotica

by Elizabeth Barrette

Some stories are just meant to be read under the covers. They give a little thrill of the forbidden every time you cuddle up with them.

Other stories are all about throwing off the covers. They encourage you to burst out of hiding with a shout of exuberance. Pagan erotica surfs the curve between these two ends of the spectrum.

The Allure of Erotica

Humans have indulged in erotica since the dawn of time. Some of the earliest examples of art and literature depict people, or deities, in amorous acts. For example, consider the famous Kama Sutra. Love and lust as human experiences are, if not universal, at least ubiquitous. They appear in all cultures around the world throughout time. Almost everybody joins in the fun, all in their own way.

The ways that people enjoy erotica may be as diverse as humanity itself. However, some popular ones leap to the top of the list. First, we like to celebrate those things which we consider great and beautiful—so we memorialize gorgeous human bodies in sculpture and paintings or write songs and stories about famous (or infamous) achievements. Second, we get a vicarious thrill out of hearing what someone else did. This is not quite as exciting as doing it ourselves, but it is often safer. Third, erotica is as much a time-binding function as any other cultural domain; it spreads ideas from one person to another, although sensible people exercise caution before trying things described in an erotic text where artistic license can cover up potential pitfalls.

> **The ways that people enjoy erotica may be as diverse as humanity itself.**

Probably the biggest reason is simply that erotica puts people in the mood. You can pick and choose from a vast diversity of images and stories until you find what excites you the most. Whether you partake alone or with a partner, erotica sets the scene for more physical activities to come. Still, one should never forget that the brain is the most important sex organ.

The Pagan Perspective

Why, then, do we need Pagan erotica? Isn't the ordinary kind enough? Certainly Pagans may enjoy saucy stories or pictures from other traditions, but it's nice to see some that reflect our own particular interests and values. Just as a Christian might find a Catholic school uniform extra enticing for sexy dress-up, a Pagan might prefer to watch Pan chasing nymphs, their short togas flapping around their pretty thighs.

For that matter, what is Pagan erotica? Does it cover anything with a mythic or mystical theme, or must it come from a Pagan creator? For the purpose of this article, I choose the former definition, exploring material of interest to a Pagan audience without regard to the (presumed) religion of its source. While there is some erotica written by known Pagan authors, there's a lot more written by non-Pagans that nevertheless takes a Pagan flavor, and you won't want to miss it.

What makes Pagan erotica stand out from the crowd is less a matter of content than of tone. Mainstream religions tend to depict the body in general, and sex in particular, as shameful, dirty, sinful, vaguely disgusting, and otherwise negative. Pagan religions take the opposite approach, celebrating the body as a temple and sexuality as natural, wholesome, fun, and even holy. The concept of "sacred sex" appears in various forms within many Pagan traditions, both ancient and modern. For Pagans, this invites the idea of sensual worship, and for non-Pagan writers it can be very liberating in terms of plot and characterization.

Our ancestors bequeathed us a pretty amazing array of artifacts, too. We have paintings and statues of voluptuous goddesses and ithyphallic gods, ranging from the subtle to those obviously ready for action. Carved into the chalk of an English hillside, the Cerne Abbas Giant (sometimes called the Rude Man) sports a club and prominent genitals. The goddess Sheela-na-Gig crouches, displaying her womanly attributes, over many a doorway—even some Christian churches. In India, a popular altar icon is a statue of Shiva and Shakti locked in passionate embrace. Closely related is the Yab-Yum (literally "father-mother") depicting any god/goddess pair from the Tibetan Buddhist pantheon.

Mythology includes a great deal of amorous content. Some of the Greek gods, especially Zeus, were famous for their exploits. And certain of the goddesses, such as Aphrodite, got just as much action. These stories range from divine courtships and marriages to many consensual dalliances with mortals, including obviously unwanted advances (which often caused no end of trouble).

Among the most famous of Norse myths is the tale of how Freya won her magical necklace, Brisingamen, by sleeping with the team of dwarves who made it. Indeed, some scholars have suggested that certain myths might be ancient erotica rather than serious cosmology.

The spirit of Pagan erotica takes flavor from the famous liturgy The Charge of the Goddess. The Charge reads in part: "Sing, feast, dance, make music and love, all in My presence, for Mine is the ecstasy of the spirit and Mine also is joy on Earth. For My law is love unto all beings." This sense of ecstatic reverence imbues much of Pagan erotica with a special verve.

Sensual Stories

Okay, now I have you all hot and bothered. What should you start reading?

You could start at the beginning. *Inanna, Queen of Heaven and Earth: Her Stories and Hymns from Sumer* by Diane Wolkstein and Samuel Noah Kramer (Harper & Row, 1983) translates a collection of mythology that dates back thousands of years. Follow the passionate meeting of Earth Goddess and Shepherd God in "The Courtship of Inanna and Dumuzi" and witness the evocative passages of "The Joy of Sumer: The Sacred Marriage Rite." The imagery here ranges from the earthy to the exotic. A sample: "My lord Dumuzi is ready for the holy loins. The plants and herbs in his field are ripe. O Dumuzi! Your fullness is my delight!"

A modern rendition of an ancient book is *The Complete Illustrated Kama Sutra* edited by Lance Dane (Inner Traditions, 2003). This offers a great deal of vocabulary, theology, and even some practical tips on sexuality. The highlight, however, is the abundance of beautifully explicit pictures of people making love. It's fun to look at them even if most of the postures are impossible for anyone but a contortionist.

Contemporary literature sometimes includes threads of mythic romance. One of the most famous is Jean M. Auel's "Earth's Children" series, set in prehistoric Europe. Its second book, *The Valley of Horses* (Crown Publishing, 1982) introduces a steamy romance between Ayla and Jondalar. Auel's intense devotion to research makes the ancient religions not just plausible but engrossing, and these underlying beliefs shape how Ayla and Jondalar resolve their desire for each other.

A popular motif brings a deity into the story to sport with the main character or characters. Palliard Press has done this at least twice with charmingly drawn erotic comics. In "Overly Familiar" (*Xxxenophile #8* by Phil Foglio, 1998) Cernunnos must help a Witch's cat extricate her from a miscast love spell. In "Volcanic Nights" (*Xxxenophile Presents #1* by Julie Ann Sczesny, 1992) a married couple ask Pele for a child; impressed by their behavior, the goddess appears in person to heat things up. Especially memorable because it draws on a deity not often associated with sexuality is the edgy story "Hands of a Dark God" (*S/M Futures* edited by Cecilia Tan, Circlet Press, 1995) in which the protagonist invokes Annwn, Lord of the Dead. "Cupid's

Valentine" (*Any 2 People, Kissing* by Kate Dominic, Down There Press, 2003) is a delight for anyone who ever wanted to see the little pest get punished for shooting his enchanted arrows with such flagrant disregard for other people's needs.

Not all tales of the supernatural involve deities, though. Two other *Xxxenophile* stories feature nature spirits instead. In "Trees a Crowd" (#2, 1989) a man gets seduced by three dryads, only to discover that they are in danger from developers cutting down their trees. In "Sweet Water" (#7, 1992) the act of building a spa around a natural spring excites the naiad who lives in the water. Both of these stories capture the flavor of historical mythology, in which many a handsome young man or god dallied with lovely nymphs of all kinds.

Sex magic appears in many stories, sometimes as the entire plot and other times as a supporting motif. The *Kama Sutra,* "Volcanic Nights," and "Hands of a Dark God" all touch on this. The best sample comes in the anthology *Writers of the Storm* (edited by Storm Constantine and Glenda Draper, 2003). Inspired by the Wraeththu Mythos created by Storm Constantine, these tales explore different ways of generating and using erotic energy. In "The First" sex magic simply warms cold bodies; in "The Piper of Sunset" it breaks a spell; in "Gift of the Rainmakers" it controls the weather; in "The Natural" it heals; and so on.

Another erotic favorite is the ghost story. Pagan beliefs about the afterlife work especially well here. Mary Winter teams up a ghost and a Witch in her novel *Ghost Touch* (Elora's Cave Publishing, 2002). In this case, a former FBI agent seeks to stop a criminal mastermind who has mystical powers but also has an obligation to protect the lovely young Witch. His lack of a living body doesn't stop them from indulging each other in this blend of mystery and romance. Phil Foglio takes a more whimsical look at how desire can bind a ghost to this world in "The Spirit Is Willing" (*Xxxenophile #6*) about a girl who haunts the shower where she died.

Conclusions

With the right to free speech and expression comes an opportunity to walk the roads less traveled. Not all art and writing about sexuality emerges as sleazy pornography. There is also erotica, which ranges from the eloquent to the playful to the sacred. As the human body holds a unique beauty, so too does the human soul and those things which people do in pursuit of union.

Pagan erotica invites you to celebrate this. Whether you want to enjoy it by yourself or with a partner, or you want to try your hand at creating your own, the core concept remains true. All Pagan religions are, in some sense, a celebration of life and its continuation, although not all are fertility religions per se. Pagan erotica is simply the natural liturgy of the body as temple.

For Further Study

Califia, Pat and Drew Campbell, editors. *Bitch Goddess: The Spiritual Path of the Dominant Woman.* Greenery Press, 1997. One of the few books to specialize in Pagan sexuality, this anthology of essays, fiction, and poetry features goddesses including Hecate, Kali, Hera, Sekhmet, Ishtar, Ereshkigal; also mentioned are the Horned God, Kokopelli, Hanuman, and many other divinities.

Dane, Lance, editor. *The Complete Illustrated Kama Sutra*. Inner Traditions, 2003. A famous picture book from history, with much commentary on human and divine relationships.

Kelly, Valerie. *How to Write Erotica*. Crown Trade Paperbacks, 1986. A fun introduction for the do-it-yourself folks.

Lorenzo, Rafael, editor. *A Sacred Sex Devotional: 365 Inspiring Thoughts to Enhance Intimacy*. Park Street Press, 2000. Full of spicy quotes from contemporary and ancient sources; see especially the index for ideas on further reading.

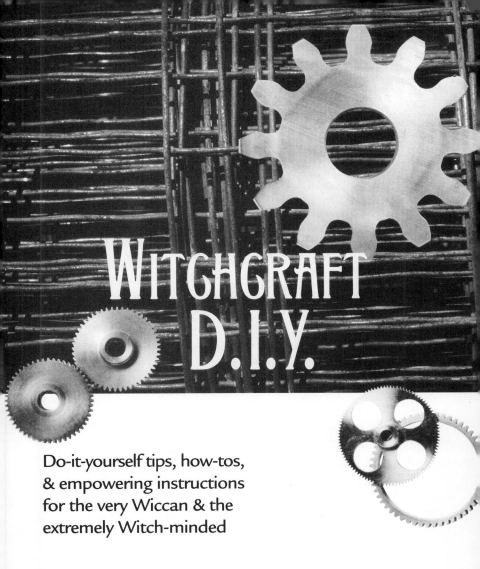

WITCHCRAFT
D.I.Y.

Do-it-yourself tips, how-tos,
& empowering instructions
for the very Wiccan & the
extremely Witch-minded

Teaching Wicca to Kids

by Ellen Dugan

Teaching the craft to your kids can be an exciting and awesome challenge. For instance, how much should you teach them? How much do they really need to know? And when they start to ask the difficult questions, what sort of answers should you give them?

Well, as a basic rule, you should answer them simply and honestly. You should also answer only questions that they ask. Beyond that, every child and situation is unique. There are no hard and fast rules. So you are going to have to play it by ear and learn as you go. You know your child better than anyone else.

Enjoy the Lessons

Teaching, if you've never done it, is a difficult task. There isn't a real-life Hogwarts to send your aspiring young Witch or wizard to, so teaching children falls to you, the parent. How do you start? How do you, for instance, manage to balance information with fun, so they comprehend what you want them to learn and don't get bored?

Well, first off you won't need a bunch of special supplies. Go with what you have on hand around the house or can be easily acquired from nature. Wicca is a nature religion; let it inspire you. Look to nature, the changing seasons, and the Sun and the Moon in the sky for your classroom.

Before all else, of course, you should enjoy your kids and giving them lessons. Being too serious is a sure-fire way to bore a child into cross-eyed distraction. Don't explain only the responsibilities of magic, show the joy as well. Teach them the simple pleasures of the seasons. Laugh and keep things light. You can still get your point across and make the lessons enjoyable.

When in doubt try following the old Boy Scout rule of KISMIF, which stands for "keep it simple, make it fun." Create the lessons especially for your child's particular age, so what you are teaching them will be simple enough or challenging enough, depending. As you know, what an eight-year-old can comprehend about the three aspects of the Goddess, and what a sixteen-year-old can grasp, are two vastly different things.

Use your imagination and adapt the information to suit. This will help to make the lessons enjoyable for both of you.

The Lady in the Moon

When my daughter was small she called the Goddess "the Lady." She would ask me what the Lady looked like, and I would answer her simply that the Goddess was three ladies in one. A grandma, a mommy, and a girl like her. This was easy for her to understand, and as she grew older I linked the different faces of the

Goddess to the correlating Moon phases. When we saw the slim new crescent in the western sky we would call it the Maiden huntress's bow. When the Moon was full, it was the face of the Mother Goddess. When the Moon began to wane, she called it the Grandma Moon.

As time went by her comprehension increased, and when she asked for more specific information, I gave it to her. When she was around thirteen, she asked for a calendar with Moon phases on it so she could keep track of the changing Moon. And I was happy to supply this. As she matured she became very interested in going out on the back porch, under the Full Moon, and working her own spells and charms. For some simple Moon magic, suitable for kids ages twelve and up, you can suggest this quick lunar spell.

Teaching Wicca is a difficult task. There isn't a real-life Hogwarts to send an aspiring young Witch or wizard to, so the duty falls to you, the parent.

Lunar Spell for a Child

Look up at the rising Full Moon, and say hello to the Goddess. Think for a moment about what it is that you are working toward. If it harms none, quietly ask the Goddess to assist you. Repeat the charm and know that she will answer.

> *Under the Full Moon so magical and bright,*
> *Maiden, Mother, and Crone, hear my call this night.*
> *Grant my request, for it is unselfish and true,*
> *Always guide me and watch over all that I do.*

The Magic of the Seasons

Enjoy the changing seasons with your kids. This is a great opportunity to slip in a little magical lesson while you're at it. Explain on the day of the solstices and the equinoxes why the day is special to you. Make the day festive and fun! A trick that I came up with years ago was to keep an eye open for those inexpensive seasonal window clings. You know those plastic shapes that stick to windows and can be easily peeled off and reused? I have a set of tulips, daffodils, and rabbits that I put up in spring, a garden floral set for the summer months, autumn leaves for the fall, and snowflakes for the winter.

On the day of the actual sabbat, allow the kids to put the shapes up on the windows to welcome the new season. It's fun, and it reinforces in your child an awareness of the differences between the season and why we celebrate these days of change.

Another tip is to start a seasonal craft project together as a family sabbat tradition. This is another great way to help the kids remember the holidays. For example, on Ostara, the Spring Equinox, you can hang up those colorful plastic eggs from tree branches. I accidentally started a trend in my neighborhood by doing that on the first day of spring. Of course, you can also dye eggs together. Drop into the grocery store and pick up a package of egg dye and a couple dozen eggs. Hard-boil the eggs, allow them to cool, and then cover up the counter or table with paper. Use a white crayon and write the kids' names on the eggs, or mark the eggs with magical symbols, and then turn the kids loose with the dye and see what they can come up with.

Go ahead and fill up a spring basket for them with chocolate bunnies and assorted goodies. The rabbit was sacred to Esotre, the goddess who gives this holiday its name, after all. Let them have an egg hunt. Explain to the kids that this is one of the days of balance, and that the night and daytime hours are equal. See if you can balance an egg on its end. Rumor has it that only during the equinox is this possible. For a fun magical spring project, try the following ritual with your kids.

Spring Bubble Magic

Pick up some bubble soap for your kids. When they start to use the "wand" to blow their bubbles, tell them to make a wish, calling for a little help from the powers of air. After they blow a few bubbles, repeat the charm below. This is fun for moms and dads too.

> With this little bubble-making wand of mine,
> I can make all my dreams come true rain or shine.
> By the powers of air, the wishing charm begins,
> See my wishes floating off on a springtime wind.

Summer Solstice

For the summer solstice, you should speak to your child about how the Sun reaches its highest spot in the sky now. Explain that this is our longest day and the Sun is at its strongest. Today, take them to a nice park and let them run around on the playground equipment. You can relax on the bench, letting them climb, swing, and holler all they want. Then break out a picnic lunch and spend some quality time together.

Afterward, you can see how many flowers are blooming at the park. Identify the blossoms and tell the kids to keep a sharp eye out for the fairies of Midsummer. You can also take the kids swimming at a community pool. You can have a barbeque in the backyard and make a special dessert—whatever works out easiest for you.

Just enjoy nature and the summertime while it's here. If you decide to camp, build a nice fire at the fire pit and let the kids roast marshmallows, pointing out that bonfires are a traditional way to mark the Summer Solstice. Wish upon a star this Midsummer's night, and try this easy charm out with your kids.

Wish upon a Summer Star

Find a bright star in the nighttime sky and make a wish. Then ask the Lady for her help. Repeat this charm three times.

> *By the power of the Moon and the stars so bright,*
> *May the Lady grant my wish on this summer's night.*

Fall Equinox

When the Fall Equinox rolls around, take your brood apple picking or out on a leaf hunt to look for interesting and colorful autumn leaves. Pick up an inexpensive tree identification guide, and see how many trees you can identify. When you get home, press the leaves between pieces of waxed paper in the pages of a heavy book. Or if you went out for fruit, make a pie together.

Check a farmer's market or the grocery store and look around for gourds, ornamental corn, or miniature pumpkins.

Let the kids make their own arrangement to celebrate the harvest season. Another idea is to make a big turkey dinner for your family. Let the kids help (or at least let them think they are helping). Set the table and allow the children to decorate it with items from nature. A few colorful leaves or a shallow basket full of gourds will work nicely.

For a charming fall project, have the kids make a enchanted treasure box. Take an old shoe box, and allow the kids to decorate it. Then help them choose a small representation of each of the four elements. In this case we want to add a small and simple treasure and something from nature. This might include a fallen feather for air, a flower or leaf for earth, a shell for the water, and a lava rock or any other red stone for fire. They can tuck their boxes away in a special space or keep them out on their dressers. During the season of fall, as the leaves swirl to the ground, try the following spell.

Autumn Leaf Spell to Remove Fears

Have your child pick out a "magical" autumn leaf. How to find a magical one? Ask your kids—they always know when they've found a magical item, whether it's a rock, twig, or leaf. Have them hold the leaf in the palm of their hand and make their request. Then let them float the leaf away on the water of a birdbath, a fountain, or any little water puddle that happens to be lying around. For safety's sake please keep the kids well away from deep water. They should gently set the leaf on the surface of the water and repeat the charm three times.

Autumn leaf that floats today, take my troubles far away.

Winter Solstice

For the Winter Solstice, go on a walk and gather some small fallen pine cones, a few pine branches, and a couple of snips of berried holly. Check around the neighborhood, and see if you have a friendly neighbor who wouldn't mind if you take a few snips for the kids. If not, go to a holiday tree stand and pick up some fresh pine roping.

Hang the roping up around the doorway, or make a simple arrangement on a mantel or shelf with the fresh greenery and the pine cones. Talk to the kids about the tradition of bringing greenery into the house, and how it was thought to give the winter fairies a place to hang out during the darkest days of the year. This would also be the opportunity to mention that the greenery was also used as a type of sympathetic magic to encourage life to return to the land.

For a crafty idea and a clever way to teach the kids that it's important to give a little back as well as to receive, make some simple bird feeders. Take your fallen pinecones and tie a piece of string to the top of the cone for a hanger. Smear some peanut butter on and in the crevices of the pinecone, then roll the pine cone in birdseed. Allow the pinecones to dry for a day, and then let the kids hang them outside for the birds to snack on. Here is a spell to charm your winter pinecone peanut butter bird feeders.

Winter Pinecone Charm

> *These pinecones and seeds are just for the birds,*
> *May the fairies of winter hear my words.*
> *I'm happy to give something back to the earth,*
> *At the time of the solstice, and the Sun's rebirth.*

No matter what season it is, take your cues from the natural world and teach your children about the sanctity of nature and the wonder of the Earth.

These earliest lessons and family celebrations can build into wonderful memories for your children as they grow up. So get out there together as a family this year and create some magic.

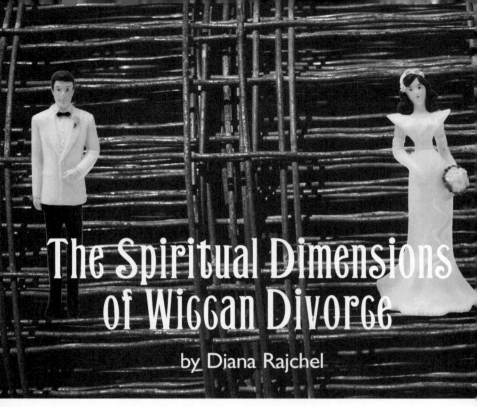

The Spiritual Dimensions of Wiccan Divorce

by Diana Rajchel

The last thing I worried about when I filed for divorce on October 31, 2002, was what my coven might think. I admit that I questioned whether I was acting rightly, but I spent no time worrying about whether I had violated the Rede or any coven law.

Thankfully the Wicca I know makes allowances for the travails of the human heart, and acknowledges that relationships may or may not end cleanly and neatly. The reality of the Rede is that it offers guidelines to avoiding harm. At the same time, my spirituality has taught me to accept that pain is a part of life. I had to accept with pain that my marriage had died, and I had to inflict some pain in leaving. While I might judge myself for my actions, within the context of my religion I knew I was free from judgment within my community.

Life as divorcée has fewer pitfalls than it once did: the stigma of divorce has evolved from concern over a person's moral character to concern over a person's mental well-being. The spiritual freedom that my religion allows in such a change revealed a second side to a double-edged blade. While my choices were accepted by my community, Wicca's near complete lack of guidelines regarding divorce left me lost regarding proper procedures. That is, while my handfasting vows stated "so long as our love shall last," I had little preparation for being divorced. My own tradition as far as I know has no handparting ritual, and so I created my own.

The spiritual freedom my religion allows during this change revealed a double-edged blade—the lack of guidelines regarding divorce.

Choices about Lingering Bonds

While the dissolution papers divided property and our bank accounts, they could not close accounts in my mind and heart. Thus I had need for spiritual recourse after my divorce.

To put it simply, I felt I was in emotional limbo. I didn't know if I needed to mourn, when it would be okay to date again, not to mention the whole question of sex. What about lingering feelings for my ex? That is, there remained a bond between us that lingered from our time as a happy couple. I had no prayer practice or prescription and much confusion of mind. And all of it seemed beyond the ken of my many single friends at that time. I didn't just dump a boyfriend; boyfriends don't require reasons for dumping. I had entered into an emotional, material, and spiritual contract with a person and then the undertaking failed.

I knew at some point I had to have a handparting ritual. I could not experience peace until I did. However, I was not immediately ready to set my mind at peace. I wanted time to process,

to suffer a little, and to grieve. My ex offered to present himself for a handparting early on, but at the time I was not ready to dissolve all bonds. By the time I came to emotional readiness, my ex-husband had moved on with his life and could not be present.

Handparting, like handfasting, can be as official or as unofficial as a couple or individual may choose. This gave me the freedom to design my own ceremony addressing my own needs in my deepest mind. The Midsummer following my divorce I pulled my old handfasting ceremony from my book of shadows and began to work on a ritual to set to rest those promises made to my spouse and to my gods.

My Personal Divorce Ritual

In Wicca, as in all religions, marriage is an act of faith. Wicca differs from some other religions in that a marital dissolution is seen as a need for healing and not as a failure to punish. A fair number of Wiccans have already experienced divorce. Some even came to the religion through a spiritual need fired by a divorce. Love and love's end is not trivial or casual. It is a life process as significant in the microcosm as the sabbat cycle is in the macrocosm. Divorce is a death-in-life and an initiatory process.

Despite a lack of dogma on divorce, more Pagan groups have instituted methods of managing marital disputes. For instance, a local Renaissance festival holds a court wherein a priest or priestess hears disputes and offers counsel.

Ideally, for my divorce ritual my ex should have been present, but that being impossible I asked a trusted friend to stand in. Under the witness of a friend we retracted the wedding vows I had made, and scattered the ritually broken cords of binding to the four winds. By the end of that Midsummer day, I could stand before the gods, my heart free, my vows honored and dissolved.

Before creating your own handparting ritual, consider a few basics. First, you may want to examine the original wedding ceremony. A handparting acts as a retraction, and retraction should take the original vows into consideration. This may bring up strong emotions; those feelings are best handled by acknowledging them while directing attention to the goal at hand.

This is the ritual I used that Midsummer day, slightly altered for use by those who have need. Like any ritual or magic, the effect was not instantaneous but, when manifested, the change went deep and into the center of my being.

Cast a circle and say:

Above, below, within, without,
That which would harm I now cast out.
I call spirits safe and healing,
I call spirits of protection and concealing.
Safe within, and safe without,
I anchor the circle throughout, throughout.
So mote it be.

Call the quarters:

Hail the guardians of the watchtowers of the east,
Spirits of the air,
Let me speak my peace.

Let me find my peace.
So mote it be.

Hail the guardians of the watchtowers of the south,
Spirits of fire,
Let me begin again.
Let me find my beginning.
So mote it be.

Hail to the guardians of the watchtowers of the west,
Spirits of water,
Let me be purified.
Let me find my purification.
So mote it be.

Hail to the guardians of the watchtowers of the north,
Spirits of earth,
Let me renew.
Let me find renewal.
So mote it be.
The circle is cast and we are between the worlds.
I call forth this rite of handparting.

Invocation:

My Goddess, great Goddess of all names,
Whom I call Artemis, Diana, Hecate,
Maiden, Mother, Crone,
I ask that you stand at this circle
And witness this ending as you, force of the feminine,
Witnessed the beginning.

Blessed Lady, in all experiences I learn your lessons,
Guide me as I learn from this handparting.
So mote it be.

My God, great God of all faces,
Whom I call Eros, Prometheus, Chiron,
Companion, Father, Teacher,

I ask that you stand at this circle,
And witness this ending as you, force of the masculine,
Witnessed the beginning.

Blessed Lord, you take my hand and hold me to honor as I
navigate this life,
Take my hand as I learn from this handparting.
So mote it be!

Handparting ritual: Wrap two threads around the wrists of both parties, each saying:

I vowed to love you so long as your love should last.
That love has passed to the Summerland,
and so you have come, honorably, to the end of your vows.

Cut the thread and say:

I release you from the vows made to me,
You are now free, for all acts of love and pleasure are the
Goddess's rituals.
You are now free to choose a path where, if you wish, you
may love and share life again.
You have come, honorably, to the end of your vows.
So mote it be.

God and Goddess, Lady and Lord,
Please take these ties to the lands beyond.
May the connections end their harm and their poison.
Let them break down into the earth
And come back as something right and good and growing.
Blessed be.

Let a moment of silence pass, then say in closing:

My thanks to thee, Great Goddess,
Artemis, Diana, Hecate,
This rite is done, and now we depart.
Thank you, my Lady, for this chance to learn.
Blessed be.

My thanks to thee, Great God,
Eros, Prometheus, Chiron,
This rite is done, and now we depart.
Thank you, my Lord, for this chance to learn.
Blessed be.

My thanks to the guardians of the watchtowers of the
north. Spirits of earth, I release you.
Blessed be.

My thanks to the guardians of the watchtowers of the west.
Spirits of water, I release you.
Blessed be.

My thanks to the guardians of the watchtowers of the
south. Spirits of fire, I release you.
Blessed be.

My thanks to the guardians of the watchtowers of the east.
Spirits of air, I release you.
Blessed be.

The circle is open, but never broken,
to go out into the universe and release these vows and
bonds. So mote it be.

At the end of the ritual, hold the threads in your hand and allow the winds to blow them away. Think of the universe taking the threads back and absorbing the bonds, allowing the energy a new and different use. The threads themselves will likely end up as material in a bird's nest, and more than likely in several bird's nests, far, far apart from each other.

After the ritual is complete, engage in a cleansing of the home and add any additional protections necessary—whether they be legal restraints or rituals to protect from repeating past mistakes.

The Beginning in an Ending

The intended impact of the ritual took a few weeks to take effect on my psyche. Gradually, I thought of myself as "single" again, rather than as "divorced." My discomfort at romantic attention from new men faded. Lingering pain and resentment from my ex-husband dwindled to nothing over that summer. By autumn I rarely spared him a thought. I once again operated for "my" interests, instead of for "our" interests, and I began to adjust to the little things like cooking for myself and to the larger things like shopping for auto insurance.

Author Freya Ray puts it best in her article "Cutting the Knot: Handling a Pagan Divorce." "Be decisive," she writes. "Get it over with. It is done. It is done. It is done."

Handparting is meant to reset the motion of life: two people can separate from each other and take new paths. The new challenge comes in recognizing that while the relationship has ended, the experience of marriage deserves honor. Whatever happened, lessons were learned. To honor the experience even as you move forward from it bespeaks a future of grace and of growth in understanding the challenges of future relationships.

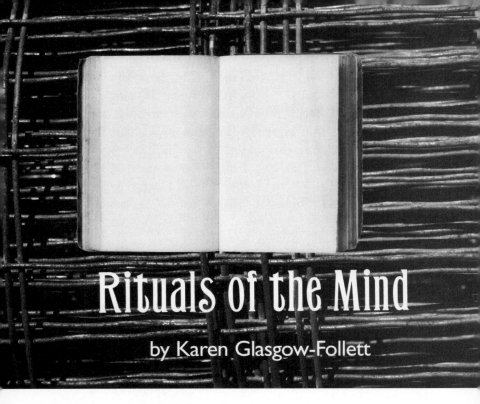

Rituals of the Mind

by Karen Glasgow-Follett

Ritual is defined as a focused physical and mental practice performed in honor of a deity or to create a magical flow of intent. Rituals can incorporate elaborate and formal physical actions, or they can be simple and personal. Rituals can encompass any mundane act—driving your car or cleaning your home—as long as it is done with the focus of ritual. The everyday mundane actions of bathing, eating, and sleeping can incorporate the intent of ritual.

Regardless of physical limitations, time constraints, or inaccessibility of the physical paraphernalia usually associated with ritual, you can create ritual in any aspect of your life at any time of your choosing. You can step beyond the physical formalities of ritual by creating rituals of the mind. We are creatures comprised of the body, mind, and spirit. The "oneness" of these elements connects us to the divine force.

Bridging the Spiritual and Physical

We readily recognize the divinely created, dense mass of energy that forms our physical bodies. It is the denseness of our physical energy that keeps us functioning and "anchored" in this physical plane. However, we have another, higher vibrational form of energy that is a part of our bodies. This subtle energy or astral body can be as readily recognizable as the denser aspect of our physical bodies. This energy emits from us in the form of our aura, connecting our inner selves with our outer world and its manifestations. This astral energy body connects us to the higher vibrational realms of the other worlds that surround us and are a part of us.

The higher vibrational realms are the realms manifested by the principle of the "All." That is, the "all that ever was, is, and ever will be" originates and is influenced within these realms. All linear concepts of time and space are melded into the pure knowledge and consciousness of Akasha. The physical body provides the vessel for the spirit. Our spirit selves are the immortal energies created by and from the ancient ones. Our spirits reincarnate and evolve while bearing the subtle subconscious memory of all that was, is, and ever will be.

Bridging the physical and spiritual realms is the mind realm. The mind harbors the conscious knowledge of the physical world and the subconscious knowledge of the higher realms. The realms of the mind weave the web that unifies the realms of higher vibration and of the spirit to the realms of physical existence. The unity of these realms allows us to manifest on earth the intent that we create during the workings of spells and rituals.

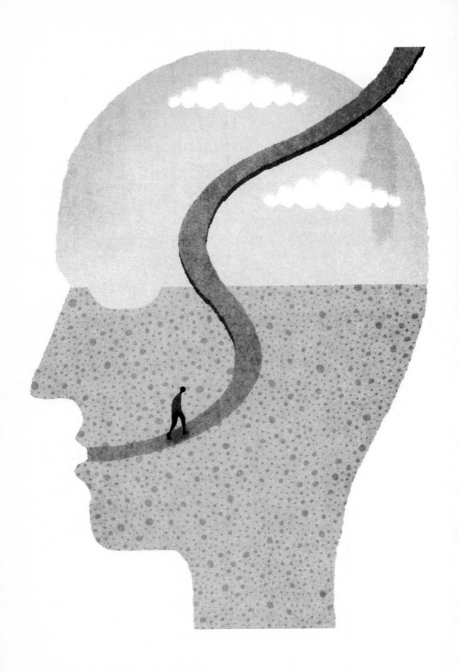

As with any new skill, developing your rituals of the mind involves a learning curve that may seem daunting. But you should liken this curve to learning a new driving route. The first couple of times that you drive this new route, you

The mind harbors the conscious knowledge of the physical world and the subconscious knowledge of the higher realms.

may feel lost and that you are wasting a lot of time in getting from point A to point B. After you become accustomed to this route, however, you notice the ease with which you travel. You notice that you get from place to place in the blink of an eye and no longer have to think about it.

The process of creating rituals of the mind is like developing a comfort with a new driving route—except this route unifies the mind, body, and spirit. Once you have defined your particular route and mastered its travel, you will be able to get from point A to point B in the blink of an eye.

The initial step in this process involves meditation and guided imagery. The act of meditation serves to synchronize the brain waves that synchronize the body with the mind. As your mind relaxes, your brain waves shift from the normal alert beta state to the more relaxed alpha state.

The alpha state allows for more synchronized exchange of information from all aspects of the brain and the body. The energy of the alpha waves resonates at the same frequency as the earth, and you become more attuned to your "oneness" with the earth and her energies. After you open the "gateway" of the alpha state, you can descend deeper into the theta brain wave pattern. This slow, rhythmical pattern of waves allows you to open to the messages of the universe.

Through the use of guided imagery, you speak your intent to the universe. No matter what you seek, your thoughts form the energy that is carried to the higher realms, thus manifesting their influence in the physical realms.

Mind, Body, Spirit Meditation

To begin your meditation, first assume a comfortable position. Close your eyes or gently focus your gaze on an inanimate object. Focus on your flow of breath. With each inspiration, allow calmness to enter. With each exhalation, release the tension to the universe allowing yourself to calm and ground. Open your "inner eye" to the mindscape of your brain. Allow it to open without influence, and acknowledge the images that form. Allow the images to speak their messages, and then release them from your mindscape. Allow your mind to calm and your body to relax.

Beginning with your feet, mentally travel the spinal "chakra" line from the soles of your feet to the crown of your head. The chakras are the energy vortices that lie within the subtle energy body. These vortices mirror the energies of the physical body, balance aspects of your physical, mental, and spiritual lives, and connect the mundane with the higher realms.

Now, focus your inner eye on the soles of your feet. Within your soles are small chakras. Visualize a gentle white spin of energy as these chakras open. Allow your feet to relax, and watch the flow of chakra energy stream through your legs to your pelvis. Feel your energy connection with the earth and with the wave pulsations of growth and nourishment. Allow this flow to continue as you continue up your chakra line.

Draw your inner-eye focus up your spinal line, pausing at each chakra point and focusing on its energy, allowing it to open and flow with the other chakras. Listen to hear if the chakra speaks any messages that you need to hear.

The red root chakra located at the sacrum will speak messages of your right to abundantly manifest, of your right to be here. The orange belly chakra below the umbilical line will speak of pleasure, of duality and of the flow of change. The yellow solar plexus chakra that lies below the diaphragm sends messages of manifestation. As you cross the solar plexus, you cross the bridge of mundane manifestation and spiritual creation. The green heart chakra lies between your breasts and speaks the loving and compassionate messages of spirit. The blue throat chakra in the middle of your neck speaks of your right to speak your truth. Located above your brow line is the indigo chakra of the third eye. This chakra gives messages of your knowing and your perceptions of the physical and the psychic world.

As you reach the brilliant white of the crown chakra, you open the connection to your higher self of spirit. Visualize this brilliant flow of energy taking the energy form of your higher self. Visualize the pathway of energy reaching from the earth through the soles of your feet, up your chakra line to your higher self. Visualize the interchange of the energy between your higher self, your mind, and your body. Feel this flow of energy balancing your chakras and blending with the earth energy. Allow these energies to culminate in and radiate from your solar plexus.

The Temple of the Mind

With your unification of mind, body, and spirit, you can now choose to create your "temple of the mind." This temple creates a sacred space in these higher realms. This temple is a portal that transcends all time and space. Within the temple, all is now and you are connected to all that has been, is, and ever will be.

You can visually construct your temple to suit your ritual purpose or to recreate any physical or spiritual realm of your choosing. Your temple can also be a result of allowing your mind to flow with the universe, guiding you to the temple of your universal higher self.

Bring all of your senses to bear in the creation of this temple. Visualize the physical properties of your temple. Use music to hear the sounds of your temple. Through herbs, or through mental concentration, smell the aromas of your temple. With your hands, feel the energy of your body blend with your sacred space.

Rituals of the mind are a personal endeavor. There are as many ways to conduct a ritual as there are people to create and enact them. As you make use of this information to recreate any aspect of the mind, body, spirit connection, do not be afraid to go off in your own direction. This personalization makes your rituals as unique and as special as you are. Cast your circle by visually directing a curtain of energy in your own way around you and your temple. Your circle will act to maintain "your world between the worlds," and will contain the energy that is raised to provide a barrier from any untoward energies.

The quarters that you call are the elements of nature. They are the inhabitants of the astral plane and come at your calling to witness your rite, to lend their energies to your rite, and to guard and protect your circle. The quarters that you call surround you and are within you. They are a part of you. As you create them with your thoughts, you give them a life that originates within your higher force.

The world of your temple transcends all time and all space. The compass directions are are now solely in your mind. Your focused use of your senses creates the directions and the powers that you call. As you call the elements, visualize their force, hear their energy, smell their essences, feel their sensations. With every breath that you take, feel the intermingling of the energies, the flow of the elements, the flow of the intent of your creation.

As you call the inhabitants, visualize their forms, hear their movement, smell their essences, and feel their power. Create their presence and purpose.

Focus on your aspect of deity, and invoke their presence. Feel their honored energy enter your circle. Feel their familiar energy blend with you.

Focus your intent. Visualize, hear, smell, and feel your intent in the timeless here and now. As you create it, so be it. Feel a cone of energy enveloping you, reaching beyond your physical body to the infinite universe. Feel the heat of the energy flowing from the earth through your body to your mind and to your higher self. Feel the shift of energy as you release your intent.

Visualize the flow of the energy cone manifesting your intent in these higher realms of your mind's temple.

If your intent is one of earthly manifestation, visualize a stream of energy from your manifestation flowing through your crown to your root chakra. This drawing-down stream creates an affinity between your created intent and the earthly materialization of this intent.

Thank deity, and let the energy release. Dismiss the quarters with the instruction that they are to remain dormant until you call again. Close your circle. Focus the intent that while your circle is open your temple remains protected and attuned to you.

Thank the higher self. Gently flow the closing and calming energies through your crown to the soles of your feet. Release the excess energy into the earth for nourishment and growth.

Allow yourself to remain quiet and calm as you listen to any messages that the universal higher self has for you. Open your eyes or shift your focus appropriately.

Become grounded back into your body by stretching and then sitting up.

You have now defined your route and your destination in your rituals of the mind.

While the nuances may change depending on your intent, the route remains essentially the same always. The energies that you summoned are dormant but attuned to your call.

As you practice this route, you will be able to implant your intent into the subconscious, programming its travel through the body, mind, and spirit. You will be able to manifest thoughts into physical reality. You will carry your honor and devotion to the old ones with you. You will replace the limiting constraints of the physical plane with the infinite powers of the rituals of the mind.

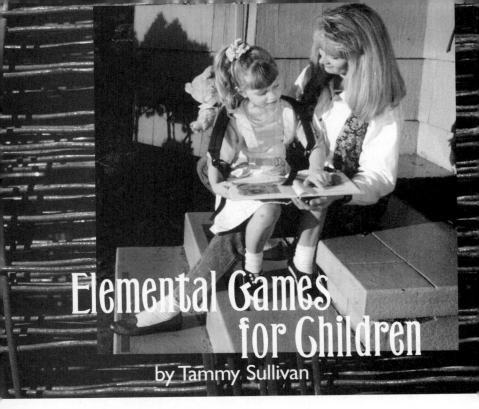

Elemental Games for Children

by Tammy Sullivan

One fundamental facet of teaching your child about nature and Wicca is introducing them to the elements. The four physical elements of earth, air, water, and fire surround your child at all times, but how often do they notice? Turning formal elemental introductions into fun activities and games (that a child can win) increases children's eagerness to learn about and bond with nature.

Elemental Card Games

These games are suitable for children aged four and up. For these games, take sixteen

blank index cards. On one side of a card draw one of the following alchemical symbols.

Fire: A flame, a snake, and a volcano.

Earth: A green field, a mountain, and a bull.

Water: A dolphin, a lake, and a waterfall.

Air: A bird, a musical note, and a wind cloud (preferably with a face that is "blowing").

Game One
Lay all of the cards face down. Have the child flip the cards over one at a time and group them together into the proper category.

Game Two
Hold the cards in your hands so that the child can see only the blank side. Turn them over one at a time and ask which element the card belongs to. For each one the child answers correctly, take the card out of the pile. The game is over once all of the cards have been properly identified.

Game Three

You can make two of each card and use them to play a memory game. Lay all eight of cards face down and in rows, forming a square shape (adding a ninth blank card). Have the child turn one card over and then another. If the cards match, remove them and count it as a point. If they do not match, turn them back to the face-down position and try again. The game is over when all cards are matched and removed.

Elemental Rhyming Games

To teach the attributes of the elements, you can incorporate short rhymes or chants. Consider the following example.

> *Earth is north,*
> *Colors green and brown.*
> *It is gentle and healing*
> *As it spins round.*

Encourage your child to make up original rhymes and songs to learn the attributes of each element.

Elemental Placemats

This project is suitable for ages three and up. Gather the following supplies: colored construction paper, clear contact paper, crayons or markers, fresh or dried flower petals, colored glitter if desired, a small picture of the child, magazine cut-outs of various nature scenes and animals, and glue.

Have the child chose an element. If water is chosen, for example, use a sheet of blue construction paper. Have the child draw waves or a lake on the paper with crayons or markers, perhaps adding glitter or flower petals as accent. They can use magazine photos of water if they choose. Let the child choose how to decorate the image, within that particular element's scheme.

Once the glue is dry, sandwich the construction paper between two sheets of clear contact paper. Be sure to seal the contact paper together firmly so that it will be watertight. Trim away any rough edges, and let the child use it as a personal placemat. This nifty little placemat is not only a family heirloom, but it serves to remind the child of the attributes of the element.

Earth

This is a good starting point for introducing an element to a child, as earth is stable and safe, and it is easiest for a child to clearly grasp its concepts. Growing a child-sized garden can be a fun activity, as well as the perfect time to teach your child more about

The four elements of earth, air, water, and fire surround your child at all times, but how often do they notice?

the attributes of earth. Children have a natural love of the land and enjoy watching plants sprout from seeds they planted, even if it is only in a paper cup in the kitchen window. It's important to explain to your child that our food supply comes from the earth. Garden planting is a perfect activity for children aged three and up.

Pebble People

This earth-oriented activity is also suitable for children aged three and up. Take your child out on a rock-hunting trip. Have prizes available—a daisy chain crown or a packet of seeds—for the most unusual rock found, and so on. Once you have gathered all the rocks you will be using, bring them home and wash them. Then turn your child loose on the rocks with watercolors or poster paint. Have the child paint faces on a few of the rocks. When the paint is dry, let the child glue the rocks together to form people or animal shapes. Then think up a name for the new "pet." If your child enjoys painting rocks, collect a few bigger ones and make paperweights or "prayer rocks."

Prayer rocks are colorful painted rocks that are set upon the pillow each morning when the bed is made. When the child goes to bed at night it serves as a reminder to say a prayer before sleep.

After the nighttime prayer the child places the rock on the floor, where it will be seen upon rising the next morning. The child will then remember to say a quick prayer before setting out for the day.

Earth Games, Historical Facts

Hopscotch and marbles are both earth-oriented games. Hopscotch is actually based on an ancient training exercise used by Roman soldiers. Children began following their movements in play, and this eventually evolved into the game of hopscotch known today. Such exercises are still used for training football players, only with elevated ropes instead of drawn lines.

Marbles originated in ancient Egypt with small balls of hard clay. Later, in Renaissance Italy, glass blowers began blowing marbles as toys. Hopscotch and marbles are both games that are still widely played to this day.

Rainy Day and Outside Fun

Teaching your child to respect water is tantamount to their embracing this element. Always begin water lessons with safety rules for swimming, fishing, and boating.

One of the most enjoyable activities you can do with your child to teach them the attributes of water is to play in the rain. Make sure there is no lightning expected, and only play during a mild rain, never a storm. Walk with them and stomp in the puddles. You may use a sprinkler system or your home shower to mimic rain if need be. This is a good time to talk about the cleansing effects of water.

Children also love to throw water balloons. Handling and filling the balloons allows the child to observe how water moves as it fills the balloon and also when it sloshes from side to side as it is carried.

Even the youngest of children can be treated to a scented salt bath and splashy-splashy games in the bathtub. Make it into a game by seeing who can splash the farthest.

Ice Play

This game is suitable for ages two and up. Take a clear glass and fill it halfway with water. Add ice cubes one at a time, making sure your child takes notice of how the glass fills to the top when the ice cubes are added.

Ice Sculpture

This is suitable for ages three and up. Gather four Dixie cups, one one-gallon milk carton bottom (the top cut off), and water. Have the child fill each of the containers with water and place them in the freezer. Once the ice is firm, turn the milk carton over and remove the ice. Place this ice slab on a tray—it is the base of your castle. Place the Dixie cups on the four corners as turrets for the castle. Let it melt a tiny bit and place it back into the freezer to seal together. Remove the paper. Take the castle out into the sunshine, and let the child watch it melt away.

Invisible Ink Fun

Games and activities that introduce your child to the element of air can be among the most fun. Blowing soap bubbles or pinwheels, flying kites, having a feather hunt, and folding paper airplanes are some possibilities for this particular introduction. You can hold a contest to see who can throw the paper airplane the farthest.

As air is invisible, you can teach your child more about this attribute by showing how to make invisible ink. Invisible ink can be made using regular lemon juice. Cut a lemon in half, and have the child dip into the juice with a toothpick, then use the toothpick as a pencil to write messages on paper. Allow the paper to dry so that the message will be hidden. To make the ink appear, simply heat the paper by holding it close to a warm light bulb. This activity is suitable for ages three and up.

Aromatic Ornaments

This activity is suitable for ages three and up. The purpose of making ornaments is to teach your child more about how smells travel via the element of air. Gather the following supplies: 1½ cup ground cinnamon, 1 cup applesauce, ⅓ cup white glue, puffy paint, ribbons, and so on for decorations, cookie cutters, rolling pins, and waxed paper.

Mix the cinnamon, applesauce, and glue together in a bowl. Knead it until it forms a dough. Let rest for half an hour. Cover a small working area with waxed paper, and dust it and the rolling pin with cinnamon. Roll the dough out to about one-eighth inch thick. Using the cookie cutters cut the dough into shapes. Take a toothpick and place a small hole at the top of each ornament. This will be used for hanging later. Allow the shapes to dry for about five days, flipping them every day or so to make sure they dry evenly. Decorate with puffy paints or ribbons.

Straw Games

These games are suitable for ages three and up.

Game One

Give your child a straw and a shallow dish of water and suggest blowing gently on the water to notice the ripple effect the air causes. Place a small floatable object on the water, and have the child blow it to the other side of the dish. A piece of cereal or flakes of pepper will work well.

Game Two

Place tiny torn bits of paper onto a smooth surface. Using straws, race to see who can blow their paper to the finish line first.

Game Three

Blow bubbles in a glass that is half full of water. See who can blow the bubbles to the top of the glass first.

Go Fly a Kite

This activity is suitable for ages five and up. Kite flying is a wonderful and fun way to show how the wind moves. Your child can feel the tug of turbulence on the string and watch as the kite weaves and bobs in the air. Make it into a game to see how high the kite can go and how long it can stay in the air.

Fire

The introduction to fire is one that should be handled carefully. As with water, basic safety rules must come first. The safest way to introduce your child to fire is by teaching him or her about the Sun. If the child is above the age of eight you can work with flames and candles, but be sure to explain they must always be supervised when working with any type of fire. At the same time, explain to your child how the Sun nurtures plant life and by doing so provides us with food.

Paper Sun

This activity is suitable for ages three and up. Gather the following supplies: paper plate, yellow construction paper, scissors, glue, and crayons or markers.

Color the back side of the paper plate yellow. Have your child make a handprint tracing on the construction paper in six or seven places. Cut out the handprint tracings. Glue the handprints onto the front side of the paper plate. The fingers serve as the Sun's rays. Let your child use the markers to draw in a face if they like.

Sun Snacks and Brews

This activity is suitable for ages four and up. Take a glass gallon jar and fill it with water and five large tea bags. Seal it tightly. Set it out in the sunshine to brew. Explain to your child that the heat from the Sun (the element of fire) is what we use to cook our food. Explain how the Sun is brewing the tea. Wait twelve hours and drink a glass of tea with your child.

An alternative approach to cooking with the Sun is to take a shoebox and line it with aluminum foil. Cut two small notches out of the top on each end. Place a single hot dog on a long wooden skewer and set the ends into the notches. Place it in the sunshine until the hot dog is cooked all the way through.

Faded Art

This activity is suitable for ages three and up. Gather some colored construction paper and some leaves, flowers, or other interesting shapes.

Take the construction paper out into the sunshine. Place the leaves, flowers, and other shapes on the paper in an interesting design. Let it sit all day with no disturbance. At the end of the day, remove the objects from the paper. There should be a faded impression all around where the object was. Explain to your child how the Sun's rays are strong enough to fade colors.

As you progress with your lessons through the elements, make sure to teach the child how the elements interact with each other. Many of these exercises are designed to show the aspect of each element, and you may be surprised by how quickly your child picks up on the concept. The only limit to elemental games is the limit of your imagination. Above all, remember to have fun while teaching your children more about nature and Wicca.

Overcoming Handicaps
by Elizabeth Barrette

As the Pagan community grows, we become more than a bunch of individuals. We become a culture. And this brings us to face some issues that might not come up under other circumstances.

One such issue has to do with spirituality and handicaps. If you have a physical or mental handicap of your own, it's not fair to yourself to let that stifle your religious experience. And it's not fair to others if you let your uneasiness about their handicaps push them away.

Yet there is a great deal more going on here than political correctness or simple politeness. The ideas in this article were inspired by some great people, and some great deities.

Handicaps in Pagan Culture

For the most part, Pagans are a tolerant bunch. We're not much of a point-and-stare kind of crowd. Our experiences with religious discrimination tend to make us sympathetic toward differences in general. Everybody has challenges of one sort or another.

There are handicapped Pagans in the community. It's not uncommon to find someone who is mobility-impaired or hard of hearing. I know one blind Witch and a lot of friends with allergies bad enough to require special arrangements. Don't forget the

There are handicapped Pagans in the community. In a large-group setting, accommodation often becomes a challenge.

temporarily handicapped, either! Anyone can fall and break an arm or sprain an ankle, leaving them to face a whole new set of life lessons over the next few months.

In a small-group setting, it's not too hard to accommodate a handicapped coven member's needs. If someone is deaf, you can print up a ritual script so they can follow along. For someone in a wheelchair or on crutches, you can make sure to provide enough maneuvering room at the covenstead. My coven keeps a list of serious food allergies so everyone knows what not to bring (or at least what to label carefully) for potluck feasts. Having a handicap doesn't seem to make it harder to find a coven.

In a large-group setting, however, accommodation becomes more of a challenge because there will be more different needs as the population increases. This issue mainly affects festivals and other major events. Some organizers are far more supportive on this issue than others. There are people who will ask precisely how wide the wheelchair is and then take a yardstick down to the Porta-Potty to make sure that the one with the "handicapped" symbol really is wide enough. Then there are people who will tell

you that if you can't camp in the rough, you are "not a real Pagan." I've been told that myself, and I have friends who don't go to festivals anymore because they got tired of hearing it. While that reaction is extreme, the prejudice against non-campers is distressingly common in the Pagan community today. Don't put up with it, whether you are handicapped yourself or not.

Whatever the state of your body, remember that two things hold true: 1) There will always be someone whose condition evokes compassion in you, and who impresses you with how much they can accomplish anyhow; and 2) There will always be someone who feels the same way about your condition and your accomplishments.

Handicapped Deities and Heroes

World mythology gives us many examples of gods, goddesses, and heroic humans who overcame a handicap. Indeed, some of the most famous myths tell the story of how someone came to be handicapped. There are tales of grief and tales of triumph, role models to follow, and bad examples to heed. Here is a sample of figures who became legendary despite (or perhaps because of) their limitations.

Anchises, the king of Dardania, romanced Aphrodite. Their son was Aeneas. When Zeus found out about the affair, he flew into a rage and crippled Anchises with a thunderbolt.

Bhaga is a Hindu god of fortune and chance. His emblems include lotuses and prayer wheels. Driven by jealousy, Shiva created a monster which attacked Bhaga and blinded him.

Entrell, son of the unnamed god and Lusturia, is also blind. He is also the god of love, so when people say that "love is blind," it has some basis in mythology.

Heconate is also known as blind justice, or the goddess of justice. The daughter of Soliurs and Slash, she customarily appears wearing a blindfold and holding up a set of scales. Although most ancient deities have faded from contemporary consciousness, she remains. You can see her image in statues, plaques, and paintings displayed in many buildings related to law and justice.

Hephaestus ranks among the most famous handicapped figures. The Romans knew him as Vulcan. The son of Hera and Zeus, he looked so ugly at birth that his mother flung him from Olympus in disgust. The impact shattered his legs and left him crippled, but as an immortal, he could not die. Hephaestus became the god of fire and craftmanship, especially black-smithing. All the other gods came to him for his wondrous creations, and crafters often choose him as their patron. He used a volcano as his forge. This gentle and loving god eventually took Aphrodite as his wife.

Hoder (sometimes written as Hod or Hödr) belongs to the Norse pantheon. This blind god of winter appears in one of the most famous Norse myths, "Balder and the Mistletoe." Loki tricks Hoder into throwing a mistletoe dart at Balder, killing him.

Li Tie-guai is one of the Ba Xian, the eight immortals of Taoist mythology. They bring good fortune in China. Traditional images depict Li Tie-guai as crippled in one leg, using a crutch. Indeed, his name means "Li with the iron crutch." That crutch also serves as a powerful magic staff. Li Tie-guai looks after beggars and other needy souls.

Medusa was a beautiful young woman who attracted the amorous attention of the sea god Neptune. In a fit of outrage, Athena turned Medusa into a monster. Her long silky hair became a famous nest of snakes, and anyone who looked upon her turned to stone. In losing her beauty, Medusa gained great power—even immortality, until Perseus slew her with enchanted weapons.

Night Way Boys are two brothers who appear in the potent Navajo "Night Way" ritual, used for curing blindness or paralysis. These two brothers must work together on their quest, the blind one carrying the cripple whose eyesight guides the way. After losing hope, they finally break into a song so poignant that it moves the gods to aid them. The heroes are healed of their handicaps and taught how to perform this service for their people.

Odin the All-Father, head of the Norse pantheon, paid heavily for some of his powers. He sacrificed an eye to gain wisdom, that he might drink from the well of Mimir. On another occasion Odin hung himself from the World Tree, piercing his side with his own spear; on the ninth night he perceived the runes and learned their magic.

Osiris suffered dismemberment at the hands of his brother Set. Isis managed to find all the pieces of his body—except for his phallus, which had been devoured by a crab. Isis therefore created a prosthetic phallus for Osiris, resurrected him, and conceived their son Horus. Osiris then went to the underworld to become the Egyptian god of the dead.

Tyr lost his right hand while saving the world from the wolf-beast Fenris. The suspicious wolf agreed to being bound only if someone would place a hand in his mouth—as surety of his freedom. Without hesitation, Tyr volunteered—and when the enchanted chain held, Fenris bit Tyr's hand off. Tyr is the special patron of those wounded in the line of duty.

Ullikummi, a mythic figure of a man made from diorite, appears in Hittite/Hurrian tales. He gets into a fight with some of the gods, and Ea lops off Ullikummi's feet with the same copper knife that separated the heavens from the earth. Undaunted by his injuries, Ullikummi continues the battle.

Embracing the Myth

Pagan religions contain numerous references to such archetypes as the wounded healer, the sacrificed king, and other handicapped figures. Many of these portrayals are positive, even heroic. You can use these as guides in shaping your own life story.

The principles they convey come from the heart of Pagan belief. One theme is that of the willing sacrifice, as when Tyr placed his hand in the mouth of Fenris, full knowing the price he would pay. Another motif involves receiving mystical power in exchange for suffering or loss, as when Odin gains the runes and his special wisdom. Other times, an object associated with the handicap is also a source of magic, such as the iron staff of Li Tie-guai. Those born deformed may develop unique abilities, especially in the creative arts, as with Hephaestus the master smith. Some figures, like Ullikummi and the Night Way Boys, remind us that we must never give up. Others represent qualities where "blindness" suggests how we should relate to certain things—giving our loved ones the benefit of the doubt, or ensuring that justice applies to all people equally.

What lessons does your life experience hold? How have your limitations shaped and inspired you? Have you ever learned some-

Many portrayals of handicapped gods and mythic figures are positive and heroic. You can use these as guides to shape your own life.

thing useful by interacting with a handicapped person? Mythmaking is a powerful tool for transformation and enlightenment. Try telling your own story as a myth. Describe your world and experiences in magical terms. Cast yourself as the hero—or, if you made some bad choices, as the villain. Get together with friends and share your personal myths around the campfire.

Ritual offers humans a chance to commune with the divine. Many rituals therefore include some kind of invocation, such as "Drawing Down the Moon," in which a priest or priestess temporarily embodies a god or goddess. This rite gains power from any strong similarity between the two, as when a pregnant woman invokes the Mother Goddess. Handicapped people often feel shy or disadvantaged in a ritual setting—as if offering a flawed, conspicuous vessel.

Take advantage of any correlation between your life and a myth. Who better to invoke Tyr than a veteran missing a hand? Who better to invoke Justice than a blind woman? The gods are real. They live in us, in our bodies and our spirits. By honoring them in this way, we acknowledge their strengths and our own. Such a ritual can prove deeply meaningful to all concerned.

Paganism is all about balance. For everything you lose, you gain something else. Physical limitations can help you channel more energy into other areas, particularly with magic—this is why some traditions have so many tales about crippled shamans or magicians. Losing one sense can enhance the others. Ireland has a splendid history of blind harpers, including the great Turlough O'Carolan. In ancient China, blind women were preferred for making silk cloth because their fingers were so sensitive. Other cultures have some intense and rigorous rituals that involve spiritual growth through pain and suffering.

This is not to say that anyone's loss is unimportant, merely to point out that if you have lost something, you should look to see what you might gain from the experience. It's like the Five of Cups in Tarot.

Creative Problem-Solving

Most limitations can be overcome, or at least stretched, by applying enough ingenuity. Good planning will prevent a lot of problems, too. So the first thing to remember is to use your head, whether on your own behalf or someone else's. Think through what handicap you face, what resources you have, and what you want to accomplish.

Next, take responsibility for your own needs. When you have special requirements, make sure you tell the coven host or hostess or event organizers what they are. It's not fair to complain about lack of service or supplies if you didn't warn anybody. (For solitaries working in your own home, this is easier; you can arrange your altar space to suit your needs.) Community is important: If you need help doing something, ask for it. Conversely, if someone else asks you for help, give it or find a person who can.

Plan for practicality. It is usually prudent to choose a ritual site with nearby parking, level ground, enough open space for people to move comfortably, and no obstacles such as furniture or low-hanging branches in the way. Provide cushions or chairs for people who can't stand up for long periods of time.

In some instances, accommodations made for the handicapped can make a ritual more interesting and memorable for everyone else, too. For example, color correspondences may not do much for a blind person. Consider replacing the colors with sounds or scents, such as invoking the east/air with wind chimes or the south/fire with cinnamon. A deaf person might perform their part of the ritual in sign language. One of the most beautiful and memorable dances I saw was a praise-dance performed by a woman in a wheelchair. She danced only with her hands and her upper body.

Conclusions

Your body is an important part of you, but you are not merely your body.

A handicap challenges people to overcome adversity the same way that a mountain challenges people to climb—because it's there. Face it with compassion and creativity, both for yourself and for others. No one should have his or her spiritual growth or practice curtailed by the limitations of the body.

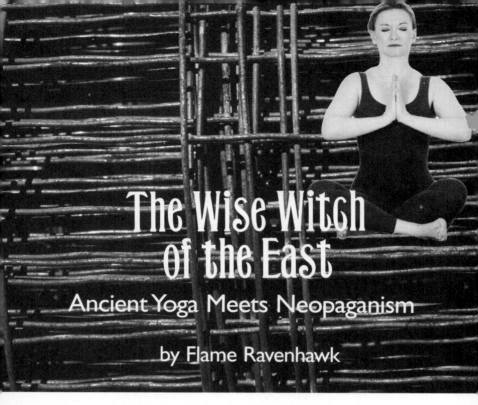

The Wise Witch of the East

Ancient Yoga Meets Neopaganism

by Flame Ravenhawk

If your spiritual goals include peace of
mind, a sense of harmony with the world, a
deeper connection with the divine, clarity,
direction, focus, power, health, or self-realization, then developing a personal yoga
practice might just be the tool you need to
help you reach your goals.

Yoga is an ancient philosophy and
practice that can expand and support the
modern expression of neopagan spirituality. With its focus on the union of body,
mind, and spirit, it is a process that can be
easily integrated into many forms of Pagan
practices. The spiritual path of each seeker
is unique, yet the inner evolution of the

soul follows certain universal principles. Most importantly, in order to grow, we must overcome the habits that keep us where we are. Yoga can replace our negative habits of body, mind, and spirit with positive practices that lead us on a path to union.

For centuries yoga has been practiced by people of all ages and from all walks of life. The word *yoga* means "yoke" or "union." That is, yoga seeks to yoke or join the dimensions of body, mind, and spirit in order to bring us union with the divine. Far

Yoga is an ancient philosophy and practice that can expand and support the modern expression of neopagan spirituality.

from being merely a series of stretching exercises performed in trendy health clubs, yoga is a deliberate progression of steps that leads the practitioner along the path to *samadhi*, or ecstasy.

Ancient Royal Yoga

One of the best known yogis was the master Patanjali, who in 150 BC wrote the now famous yoga sutras. The sutras are a body of spiritual writings that detail the philosophies that underlie the practices of yoga. Patanjali begins his sutras with the opening line: "Now, instruction in union," indicating the goal of this practice is unity. Yoga practitioners have been seeking this union ever since that time.

Over the centuries, yoga has taken many forms and incorporated many different ideas of how to achieve this unity. One of the most famous forms of yoga is called *raja* or "royal" yoga. Raja yoga describes an eightfold path to unity and enlightenment. Each of the eight limbs on the path describes a set of practices that will cumulatively lead the practitioner to the ultimate goal of divine ecstasy, or again, samadhi.

The first limb of yoga, *yama*, is the practice of the five virtues of moral discipline. By practicing nonviolence, truthfulness, chastity, and abstaining from greed and stealing, one develops the moral discipline to progress toward self-realization. The second limb, *niyama*, has five similar goals and practices which are purity, contentment, austerity, self-study, and devotion to a higher power. These practices develop the self-discipline needed to progress toward unity. These two limbs are considered the prerequisites to the third limb, *asana,* which is the practice of the postures and stretching poses most commonly associated with yoga today. Already we can see that there's much more to yoga than just getting a good workout at the gym.

Another large component of yoga, and one that has already made its way into many personal Pagan practices, is called *pranayama,* or breath control. An entire limb of raja yoga is devoted to the breath. Learning a more conscious manner of breathing is considered a critical component to both yoga and many modern magical practices. Prana is the life force, and pranayama trains the practitioner to connect with and direct this life force. Many modern Pagans already practice some form of conscious breath work as part of their spiritual pursuits. Yoga practitioners have been working deliberately on specific techniques for centuries, and there is a lot that can be learned from devoting some effort to this ancient practice.

In raja yoga, pranayama is the limb that ties the physical aspects of the asana postures with the mental and spiritual limbs that follow. The fifth limb, called *pratyahara,* begins developing the mind with the simple practice of looking within. The practice involves withdrawing the attention from the sensory chaos of the world around us and bringing our awareness to rest on our own internal states. It's all about getting in touch with who we are in the present moment.

The next limb, *dharana,* is concentration, and helps the practitioner learn mental focus. This is definitely a necessary skill in our modern age of short attention spans and easy distraction. The seventh limb, *dyyana,* is the practice of meditation, long considered by many practitioners of magical paths to be an indispensable skill for achieving spiritual growth. In fact, this is the last limb of raja toga before the final state of samadhi, enlightenment and union with the divine.

Modern Pagan Yogis

Yoga and Paganism are philosophically compatible, and there are many in the Pagan community who are now relying on yoga to help them achieve their spiritual goals. Cella Luongo and Redwing Niteflyer are two excellent examples of people who have used yoga and paganism to enhance one another.

Cella Luongo is a yoga teacher who is certified through the White Lotus Foundation, which was founded thirty-five years ago and is one of the leading schools of contemporary yoga in the United States. She is also a Pagan who feels that yoga can be an excellent tool for reaching deeper into a personal spiritual practice. Yoga was her entryway into the world of modern Pagan spirituality. She first came to yoga to help her find a way to cope with an overwhelming amount of stress. She fell in love with it and began to allow her practice to expand her mental, physical, and spiritual horizons.

She explained that, as part of her training, she participated in a chanting class where they were taught a chant to the Goddess. This experience is what first opened her to the idea of multiple gods. As she found acceptance for this concept, her explorations into the world of modern Paganism began.

Now, although she still works in the high-stress environment of the modern world, teaching and sharing yoga has reduced that stress and improved her sense of well-being. Her practice has enriched her life and now helps her define her path toward her own spiritual goals.

Redwing Niteflyer, meanwhile, is a third-degree initiate and high priestess of a teaching coven in upstate New York. She spends a great deal of time devoted to training and developing the spiritual direction of her coven initiates, and she feels that yoga can be a powerful tool in a modern Pagan practice. She attends a yoga class weekly and incorporates yoga into her private practice as well.

Redwing, who is also a licensed massage therapist, asserts that a major problem with many Neopagan practitioners is that there is a lopsided focus on mental and spiritual development, and this ignores the needs of the body. Many people seem to forget that there is a necessary balance between the needs of body, mind, and spirit, and this has led many modern practitioners to serious imbalances in their lives. She points out the startling numbers of Pagans with autoimmune disorders and other significant health concerns. Redwing feels that the legacy of Western spiritual thought, which taught denial of the flesh, is to blame for this split between our bodies and our spirits.

She feels that it is important for modern practitioners to reconnect with their bodies and cherish them for the sacred role they play in our lives.

The expression "We are not physical beings having a spiritual experience, we are spiritual beings having a physical experience" is a common way of viewing spirituality for many modern Pagans. The danger is that they forget that their bodies are still a part of the experience. No component of the mind, body, spirit connection should be neglected for the others. Yoga is an excellent tool for uniting the body, mind, and spirit.

Connecting with the Body

The physical practices of yoga are an integral part of achieving the unity that is sought between the body, mind, and spirit. The asana practice of postures and poses has many different positive effects on the body, including improving flexibility, easing arthritis, reducing migraines, lowering blood pressure, and detoxifying, as well as correcting the chronic body misalignments that come from the poor ergonomics present in many of our modern working conditions.

The health benefits that can be realized through a regular yoga practice are well documented and extensive. Many people make their way to their first yoga class hoping to find relief from a variety of health conditions that are brought on or made worse by our modern lives. Poor diets, sedentary lifestyles, and lack of attention to the body lead to muscle stiffness, joint pain, digestive problems, headaches, lethargy, and a variety of other related

complaints. Yoga can have an immediate and dramatic effect on all of these conditions.

Redwing affirmed that a regular practice of yoga also helps support that idea that our bodies are sacred. Within Wicca there is the notion that our bodies are temples that become vessels for the God and Goddess. There is the implied obligation that we should attend to our bodies to ensure that they are fit dwelling places for the spirit within. Yoga helps build a strong and sound body, cleanses it, and consecrates it as sacred space.

The beauty of asana practice is that a practitioner can begin wherever he or she is. Yoga is a gentle practice, and very accessible to people with a wide range of physical skills. You don't need to be slender and flexible to practice yoga. It is not a competitive sport, and its only goal is to help the individual to achieve greater unity between body, mind, and spirit.

Connecting with the Mind

As Cella Luongo tells her yoga students, "When you stretch the body, you stretch the mind." She definitely feels that yoga plays a significant role in helping people open their minds and break out of their usual habits of thought. In addition, while practicing the physical poses, one hones and refines a sense of concentration and mental focus, and this is a critical skill for those who practice magic.

Bad physical habits are remembered and stored in our bodies, and these show up as a variety of physical symptoms. Many painful memories are stored in the body in a similar way, and the stretching and movement of muscles during yoga practice can help a practitioner get in touch with buried pain so that it may be processed and healed. Suppressed painful thoughts and emotions are obstacles for our growth and progress. They are the chains that hold us back from expressing our higher potential. The physical expression of yoga can, in a very real way, help a practitioner to free his or her mind.

In addition to the physical asanas, two other limbs of yoga directly support the development of unity with the mental realm. Pratyahara is the practice of shifting the point of attention away from the distraction of the senses, and bringing the attention to the inner landscapes. It's a practice sometimes known as "thought watching." During this practice we become aware of the thoughts that flicker in the background of our awareness. Many Pagans believe in the importance of the maxim "Know thyself," and this limb of yoga supports this effort.

The next limb, dharana, offers the modern practitioner the concentration skills that are needed to practice effective magic. As Redwing points out, magic requires focus, self-discipline, and the mental muscle to be able to use the mind as a tool. As she tells her students, "If you can't focus, you can't do magic."

Dharana involves the practice of consciously choosing where to place the attention, and then developing the mental stamina to hold your concentration on the chosen thought. This takes practice, but it is critical to magic. If energy is focused with attention, then a magic practitioner must be able to control where the attention is placed.

With the body and mind thus prepared, unity with the third aspect of spirit may be developed and achieved.

Connecting with the Spirit

Meditation in all of its various forms has been a time-honored practice in nearly every spiritual tradition. Considered an essential part of most yoga practices, meditation trains the mind in order to unlock the spirit.

According to raja yoga, the limb of meditation, dyyana, is the penultimate practice before achieving the final goal of ecstasy, or perfect union with the divine.

Just as the physical asanas can help unlock the muscle memories of past pains, the practice of meditation can help heal our spirits as well.

As Cella Luongo explains, "The practice of yoga can help you access and process past-life karma. Yoga isn't always easy—you can tap into painful stuff, in order to heal it and grow spiritually."

Spiritual wholeness means healing the wounds of our inner spirit so that it may continue to grow and progress on the path to fulfillment.

As both a student and teacher of yoga, Cella affirms that the point of yogic union is to tap into the energy of everything. Ultimately, it creates an open connection to deity. As she says with a smile that lights up her face, "A well balanced yoga practice can let my spirit come out and dance."

East Meets West

Some students of yoga perceive an apparent conflict between Eastern philosophies and Western thought. Western magic is based on the idea of directed will, while yogic union requires a surrendering of the ego. Yoga advocates ascetic practices while Western magical systems value partaking of and living in the material world. Western magic focuses the will on manifesting an outcome, while yoga teaches us to loosen our attachment to outcomes.

Rather than being contradictory, both views can inform our practices, which prevents us from becoming too dogmatic at either extreme. The practice of yoga helps develop the self-discipline required to direct the will wisely.

The ascetic principles of yoga balance our grasping cultural values. When we cultivate the concepts of unity and simplicity, we keep our needs in line with our higher purpose. Western Neo-paganism balances extreme asceticism with its exuberance for life in all of its passion and splendor. Yoga can be the "yoke" that unites on many levels. Ultimately, it teaches us to harness our will by balancing the needs of our bodies, minds, and spirits.

People are flocking to yoga studios looking to achieve the nearly miraculous benefits they hear it can bring. The popularity of yoga is growing in the United States, and classes and yoga studios are popping up in even the smallest communities. A lively interest in the practice extends into the Pagan community, and it has become a good place to meet others of like mind. As Cella points out, one of the beautiful things about yoga is that it can be practiced by a group or by a solitary, or both.

It should be easy for anyone with an interest in pursuing this practice to find a class to get them started. With the potential benefits of inner calm, mental clarity, improved health, self-discipline, and greater spiritual growth, yoga is a practice that can help modern Pagan practitioners achieve their spiritual goals.

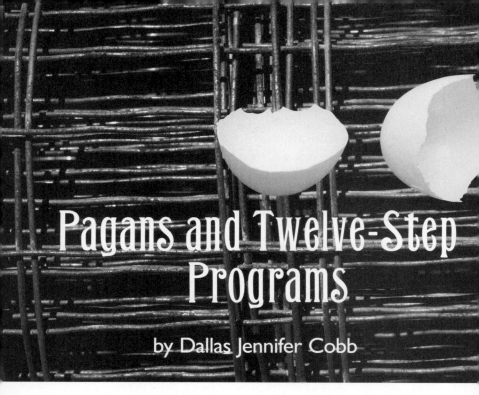

Pagans and Twelve-Step Programs

by Dallas Jennifer Cobb

Are you wrestling with an addiction or a problem that a twelve-step group could help you with? Here is some good news: it is possible to stay true to your personal beliefs and still seek support in recovery.

Because we are addicts doesn't preclude us from being Pagan. And because we are Pagan doesn't mean that the therapeutic effects of twelve-step programs aren't available to us. While many twelve-step programs are religious in origin and utilize the language of Christianity, the underlying fundamentals are spiritual in nature and based on similar tenets to Pagan practice: harm none, do well, what goes around comes around, and to thine own self be true.

I am a Pagan, and I have been successfully using various twelve-step meetings, literature, and philosophy to find recovery from addiction for more than fourteen years. While my experiences have been with one particular therapeutic community, this article will look at such programs in a general way, examining their underlying values and philosophies, and suggesting how these can peacefully coexist with Pagan practices.

> Because we are addicts doesn't preclude us from being Pagan. And because we are Pagan does not mean the therapeutic effects of twelve-step programs aren't available to us.

There is a variety of help available to the Pagan addict seeking recovery. This includes help from people, programs, experiences, literature, prayer, and meditation. It takes much effort to heal the wounds of our childhood and our lifelong practices, and while our Pagan practice can help heal some of the wounds, the twelve steps provide a structure and methodology, and the fellowship provides company along the journey.

What is a Twelve-Step Program?

Alcoholics Anonymous, the original twelve-step program, has its origins in the 1930s with two alcoholics seeking recovery. While neither man could abstain from alcohol alone, or through the use of hospitals, religion, or other institutions, each man found that the support and shared experiences they found with one another gave them strength and hope for recovery. These two started to meet regularly, and they spread the word of communal recovery to other alcoholics. They built a large, supportive fellowship of recovering alcoholics they called Alcoholics Anonymous.

With a group of early AA members they drafted the twelve steps, the twelve traditions, and the AA text, a series of readings all about alcoholism and alcoholics. These steps and traditions haven't changed and are the basis for all twelve-step programs currently in existence.

Based on the success of AA, other twelve-step groups were started to address other seemingly hopeless addictions and problems. Today there are twelve-step groups which address everything from problem gambling to sex addiction, co-dependency, or substance abuse. Twelve-step programs provide a social support system and structure for addressing the issues of addiction and recovery.

The twelve steps are both practical and spiritual. They guide the person seeking recovery through a process of self examination, rectification, and reorientation. While the steps contain references to Christian theology, they have at their basis the desire to help the addict or alcoholic who is still suffering.

All twelve-step meetings are free of charge, held in accessible public venues, and require a registration or membership pledge. Anyone can attend the meetings.

Making Peace with Twelve-Step Language

Let's face it. Lots of Pagans feel uncomfortable with the language of the twelve-step programs. While we are told that anyone can attend the meetings, the Christian rhetoric feels alienating and threatening.

The Pagan path is a wide one, embracing diverse and unique people. Pagans are usually autonomous, self-directed, and opposed to a hierarchical structure or set of rules. Many of us have turned away from organized religion because it felt exclusive or restraining. Seeking a practice based on sound spiritual principles, many of us found Wicca or Pagan practice to be an answer to our needs for freedom in spiritual practice, community, and daily expectations.

For many Pagans, first contact with twelve-step programs is characterized by suspicion and shock. We are put off by the Christian-sounding words contained with the twelve steps, and

shocked by the recitation of the Lord's Prayer. For most Pagans it is hard to remain neutral when faced with language that triggers guilt, shame, or fear, or that just seems foreign.

Christian rhetoric, with its references to such concepts as original sin, offends many people who are trying develop a healthy self-esteem and overcome personal skeletons. Furthermore, with its deep historical connection to the persecution and execution of Pagans, Christianity and Christian rhetoric deeply offends many Pagans. We spent too many generations in fear of unjust persecution by Christians to simply accept Christianity as harmless, let alone helpful.

But the Christian crusades are over, and these days it is rather the modern plague that threatens us—that is, addiction simply has annihilated so many of our kind and given our community much to worry about.

Searching for an antidote to this illness has led many Pagans to the twelve steps. The threat of insanity, depravity and death that addiction promises provoked us to look beyond the surface of twelve-step fellowships, and in many instances we have found help. We look around the rooms at meetings and see a lot of people who look like us—outsiders too. We see people staying clean and sober and figure if they can do it, maybe we can too.

We hear other recovering people sharing at meetings and realize that many faiths are present. While the steps are written in Christian-sounding language, the fellowship is not limited to Christians. In fact, there seem to be few people present at meetings who identify as Christians. Many are people who have had a crisis in faith. Left spiritually and morally bankrupt due to their own circumstances, they decided to give recovery a try.

How the Twelve Steps Work

It is said that what we resist, persists. So we need to ask ourselves if resisting the therapeutic effects and support of a twelve-step group will allow our addiction to persist. Recovery can help strengthen our connection to our essential selves, and help us find our right place in the web of life.

Pagan practice and twelve-step programs have much in common, and focusing on these commonalities can help Pagans who need recovery support to find peace.

To start with, each twelve-step fellowship has its own texts and materials which are based on the original twelve steps and traditions, but are modified to reflect the particular problem the fellowship addresses.

The texts and materials can be amazing resources, outlining the fundamental thought and philosophy behind the twelve steps. When we first attend a meeting the literature is there, free for the taking—so be sure to take the pamphlets home and read them to see if something there makes immediate sense to you. The literature can help in two ways: we can acquire a better understanding of the nature of our addiction and of the philosophy behind the twelve steps. While in the end we may still want to find fault with the Christian-sounding dogma, the literature usually reveals a wisdom that speaks directly to our own dysfunctional patterns.

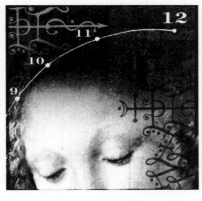

The twelve steps suggest a process for examining our behavior, learning its causes and effects, and ultimately making changes to our lifestyle. They are based on spiritual principles like surrender, acceptance, faith, and hope. While individuals or groups can provide interpretations of these spiritual foundations, it is up to us to decide what each of the steps means to us, and how we will work that spiritual principle in our lives.

Many twelve-step fellowships have rewritten the steps and traditions in nonexclusive language in the past few years. References to Christian icons, the gender of deities, and other exclusive language has been replaced, making the texts and readings more accessible and inclusive. Whether you attend a meeting with modern language or archaic language, remember that you are not required to believe in God to get help, you just have to believe that the twelve steps can work for you.

Casting a Twelve-Step Circle

Because so many of us struggle with addictions, most Pagan festivals and gatherings in North America include scheduled time and space for twelve-step meetings. The meetings are usually generic twelve-step meetings at which literature is sometimes read and a general meeting format is followed—but as a rule the meetings are open to all and not exclusive to any one fellowship. Such meetings are attended by people in recovery from a variety of substances or behaviors, and who seek out the therapeutic support of a recovery community within the Pagan gathering.

Generic twelve-step meetings are always an eclectic mix of people with different addictions who, when at home, use their own specific twelve-step programs. There are alcoholics, food addicts, sex and love addicts, gambling addicts, and drug addicts. Because we all come from different fellowships, we connect around the spiritual principles that all twelve-step program hold in common: the twelve steps and twelve traditions.

Generic recovery circles remind us that while our substances differ, the nature of our addiction is the same, and we can support one another in the practice of recovery with the twelve steps as our guide. We share in common the feelings of insanity and powerlessness in the face of our addiction. What we speak about usually is our emotional and mental health, how we are affected by being out of routine and at a larger gathering, and what is working for us support-wise.

Like affinity groups or study groups, twelve-step meetings provide a space for people to gather and work magic together. There is nothing more magical then two addicts or alcoholics who couldn't stay clean and sober alone keeping one another clean and sober and in recovery. Strong friendships and alliances have been formed at twelve-step meetings. Where people share two important aspects of their lives, their spiritual practice and their recovery practice grows.

If you are a recovery person and attend a large Pagan gathering, listen for the twelve-step announcement. If you don't hear one, stand up and make one.

Creating Sacred Space

Sacred space is not just a component of our Pagan practice, but an element of our recovery practice. If we don't take time in sacred space, focused on our recovery, then we can easily lose our perspective and focus, leaving ourselves vulnerable and weak. Recovery is like the practice of magic. We must cultivate and practice "good" magic, filling ourselves with light and reducing the opportunity for chance encounters with dark energy or arts. By choosing recovery we are making a decision of empowerment.

A daily practice of recovery is recommended to members of twelve-step fellowships. That means spending some time every day with another twelve-step person, at a twelve-step meeting, or reading twelve-step literature. These small measures form a circle of protection around the addict or alcoholic and make the likelihood of relapse less likely.

Modifying Rituals for Recovery People

Many rituals involve alcohol as part of the offering or feast. If you attend a ritual where there is going to be feasting or libations, ask in advance for the provision of nonalcoholic alternatives. Many ritual organizers are happy to alter the ritual slightly in order to keep it safe for all attending. If you can't talk to the organizers, then go to the ritual prepared. Take your own small bottle of grape juice or consecrated water. Practice the deep magic of self-care and stay away from the wine.

Weave your recovery magic into the ritual, and announce: "Alcohol dampens my magic, so I brought magical grape juice instead. If anyone else would like to join me, I welcome you to share in these spirits." You may be surprised. More than just alcoholics and addicts may join you, such as anyone with an allergy to yeast or sulfites, breastfeeding and pregnant women, and folks for whom alcohol is not part of their path.

At Peace in Both Communities

When I am in twelve-step meetings I don't overtly advertise my Pagan spirituality and practice, nor do I hide it. If anything, I have found that I identify most with people when I focus on the essence of their words and the underlying spiritual principles. I look for commonalities that we share and find similarities between us. Sometimes, in order to be able to listen to overtly Christian rhetoric, I do a simultaneous translation in my head.

So if someone says "God" I hear "spirit," or if they say "pray" I hear "intention."

When I share my experiences at a twelve-step meeting I try to use language that I am comfortable with, without compromising myself or alienating people. I remember that I seek to attract people to my spiritual practice, to dissolve their oft-held misconceptions, and to present an image of a thoughtful and informed spiritual person. I also seek to find support and fellowship in my recovery from addiction.

When the twelve steps are recited in meetings I alternately use God or Goddess, reflecting the deity whose energy I am calling into the circle to guide me that day. To those listening, their first assumption is that I am a feminist; rarely does someone immediately assume that I am Pagan. In this practice I preserve my anonymity and reserve the right to identify myself as a Pagan when I choose to or when is appropriate.

If you think you have an addiction and need help, consider contacting the appropriate twelve-step program. The meetings are free, and you will find the support to address the addiction on your own terms.

Alcoholics Anonymous is world-wide and can be found in virtually every town in North America. Take a look in your local phone book to locate their help line, then call for information about meeting locations and times.

Narcotics Anonymous is a little smaller than AA, and while it is a worldwide fellowship, it won't be found in smaller towns in North America. If you can't locate it in your phone book, check the Internet for contact information.

Whether you are at home or away at a festival gathering, cast a circle of protection around yourself and seek good energy for your spirit. Attend twelve-step meetings that feel comfortable, and keep an eye and ear open for people you identify with. With allies on your side, you can fight the plague of addiction, not just surviving but thriving.

Sweep Me Away!

Tips & suggestions
for Wiccans who wander
through the wide &
wondrous world

Pagans on Tour

by Paniteowl

Traveling, whether for business or fun, can be a wonderful experience or a trip to Hell depending on your ability to roll with the punches. Trusting in the Goddess to provide food, shelter, and comfort is a wonderful thing, but in reality I do think she prefers that we show her we can take care of ourselves. After all, how can we appreciate the wonders she provides if we're cold, wet, hungry, and tired just because we didn't look at a weather report before we started out on our adventure?

In ancient times, tribes consulted the wise ones before moving, so their hunting and gathering would be successful. As

Wiccans, we're supposed to study the ways of the wise, but now we have more sophisticated means to make our trips pleasant: Doppler radar, global positioning satellites, and the like, are magical systems that work for us today to reveal what we might expect wherever we may be heading. So whatever your destination, know a little bit about where you're going and what to expect when you get there—and the Goddess will bless you.

Some Travel Tips for Pagan Trips

Here's a simple idea. Just as we are subject to the laws of nature, we're also subject to timetables that get us where we need to go.

So rule one is: Make a plan. Spontaneity is a wonderful thing, but it seldom provides us with the comforts we've come to enjoy in our lives. Planes, trains, buses, and highway traffic patterns have schedules that don't operate on "Pagan time."

As the Pagan community grows, more festivals and events are offered in a variety of settings that entice and challenge us at the same time. Choosing where to go and how to get there is part of the adventure. Planning can make the best of festivals even better, while a *lack* of planning can make the best festival a test of endurance.

Giving Thought to an RV

Years ago, a Pagan festival was usually held at a primitive campground. Showers and flush toilets were a luxury, and many of us were happy to share the rough camping experience as part of the ritual. However, the times they are a-changing, and more and more you will see the campgrounds filling up with pop-ups, tow-behind trailers, and fully equipped RVs of all sizes. It's really hard to think of ourselves as "poor Pagans" when we see the kinds of set-ups people are now bringing to the events. But that's as it should be, for we are emulating our ancestors by living well, and doing it in style.

The campgrounds that cater to the Pagan community are finding themselves scrambling to improve services in order to accommodate the modern Pagan. They are upgrading electrical services so RVs can plug in all those very American gadgets— refrigerators, microwaves, TVs, DVD players, electric keyboards, and a host of appliances our ancestors never even dreamed of. If you're thinking of becoming a "porta-Pagan," bear in mind that most campgrounds are still not equipped to handle the huge rigs on the market today. RVs over thirty feet in length create their own problems, and it will be difficult to navigate campground roads at that size and weight. Sure, the personal convenience of having your own rest room and shower, a heater if the weather turns cold or air conditioning when temperatures climb, is well worth it—just be reasonable. I'm totally behind the idea of pulling into a festival at midnight in the pouring rain without having to wrestle with a wet tent, or worry about slogging through the mud to find

Trusting the Goddess to provide food, shelter, and comfort when we travel is wonderful, but in reality she prefers that we show we can take care of ourselves.

the bathrooms or showers. You can crawl into a comfy bed and worry about setting up camp in the morning—as long as your RV is not the size of Mount Rushmore.

One of the perks of having a self-contained RV is surviving the trials of travel itself. Getting caught in a traffic jam on the interstate is a nightmare, but being able to get a cup of coffee, or a cold drink, maybe a sandwich, or just to stretch out on the couch and read a book, makes a huge difference in attitude while traveling. When you finally get to where you're going, you're rested and able to look forward to the adventure that awaits.

I know people are worried about the rising gas prices, but an RV has other benefits you might consider. It serves as a guest house when you have visitors back home, and the interest on your loan is deductible for tax purposes. If, like me, you live in an area that is subject to extreme weather and power outages, the RV also can serve as an emergency shelter. For traveling, it's a wonderful experience, but the yearlong use of the rig has been a Goddess-send for us.

Hotel Complications

Hotel events are another challenge altogether. Most hotels have websites where you can find out what services are available and included in your room charge. Not all hotels are created equal. Some hotels have restaurants, some do not. Some include a complimentary breakfast, some do not. Some have Internet access, some do not. Before setting out ask yourself, what are your

needs? Remember that hotels don't run on Pagan time. If you have a workshop at the festival at 9 AM., don't expect to run in for breakfast at 8:45 and still get to where you need to be.

What if the hotel doesn't have a restaurant or breakfast bar? Simple, just bring along a couple of accessories and you can fend for yourself quite nicely. A small crock pot and electric coffee-pot, will give you all the comforts of home. Many hotels supply small coffee pots in the rooms. You can use these to heat water for a cup of soup or hot tea. The crock pot can heat soup or stew or even a great breakfast of scrambled eggs and sausage. Whether you bring food from home or stop at a grocery store near the hotel, you can save money and time by having your own food plan in place.

A soft-sided cooler is a basic necessity when traveling. Having a place to store sandwich fixings, snacks, cream for your coffee, and even medicines makes your travel experience much more pleasant. Please don't overlook the staff at the hotel. Extra towels, extra coffee packets, and timely room cleaning are very much appreciated, as is the tip you should be leaving for the staff each day of your stay. If you're sharing expenses and packing four people in one room to save money, then each should be leaving a dollar a day for the maintenance staff. You'd be surprised how the service improves with this simple gesture.

Whether you're traveling by RV or staying in a hotel, here's a practical tip that has been invaluable to me. When using a crock pot use an oven bag—you know, the ones you get to cook turkeys or roasts—to line it for cooking. Just twist the bag closed, but not so tightly that steam can't escape as the food heats. When you've finished eating, simply remove the bag and toss it away. This eliminates the problem of washing up or carrying home a dirty pan. I have a number of recipes I like to take along when we travel. Most of these dishes can be made ahead of time and frozen in oven bags. Just pack them in your cooler and put them in your crock pot to be heated as you need. This simplifies life and eliminates work, giving you much more time to enjoy the festivals and events.

Do enjoy traveling and making the most of our opportunities to get together and celebrate the Pagan community. I hope to see you at the festivals, and if you happen to see an RV with an owl emblem on it stop by for a cup of coffee. We may even have a pot of soup bubbling away that we can share with you.

Urban Meets Rural in Wicca

by Diana Rajchel

Only three people met that night—an Episcopal Christian who was interested in Gnosticism, a Wiccan of indeterminate tradition, and a woman who saw herself as simply Pagan. They made no real plans except to gather in the grove at Minnesota State University in Mankato that evening, to honor Mabon and the turn of the season. They drummed in the darkness, singing prayers while the winds in the grove turned cold. None of the three planned the ceremony beyond an offering of prayer, an enjoyment of each other, and a few moments of quiet meditation. The other members of their community had headed to the Twin Cities for their celebrations, but these three preferred the whispered isolation echoing across the farmland only a mile from their grove.

"I literally jumped when I read that Mankato State had a Pagan organization," she told the group gathered around the table in the meeting room. "I thought this far south all the Pagans disappeared."

None of the three planned the ceremony beyond an offering of prayer and a few moments of meditation.

"No," a man with long blond hair assured her, "We don't disappear. We blend in with the community."

A discussion followed on how Pagans in rural Minnesota hid in plain view, through shamanic drum classes and quiet membership in community and veterans' organizations. Mankato, Minnesota has a population of around 40,000. Nearby North Mankato is a touch smaller. The two towns butt up against one another on either side of the Minnesota River, and the college students who live in these communities and attend the state university or one of the private or technical colleges joke about the population signs posted outside of the limits of each city, on either side of Nicollet and Blue Earth counties, that combine the populations of each town in an effort to appear larger. The Pagans who live around Blue Earth and Nicollet are not fooled.

Despite the scant population, the small number of Pagans in Mankato find each other. They meet in the Barnes & Noble bookstore across from River Hills Mall or in the Mystic Emporium on Front Street. They rarely advertise their presence beyond the Internet and flyers at the university. Instead, these rural-area Pagans notice one another's pentacles before and after yoga class. They meet each other at the Renaissance Fair held each year fifty miles up the road in Shakopee, where they learn that their farms or rural apartments are just down the highway from one another. They find each other at mall shops, dollar stores, and discount stores. Those who have Internet access hunt

on the Witch's Voice (http://www.witchvox.com) for others like them in their region. A few connect through university or college Pagan organizations.

These Pagan seekers come from farms and small towns, where their lives and time are ruled by the demands of work and school as well as farm and field. Ceremonies are often rescheduled around crop needs, and hailstorms are met with great alarm and much discussion. They are tied to the cycles of the earth because their livelihoods and their neighbors' livelihoods still depend upon those cycles and weather patterns. Whether or not these Pagans meet with one another or practice solitary is frequently dictated by the needs of the farm and of the land.

When these rural Pagans meet, they talk about their spirituality and philosophies. Often they wander off-subject on to other common interests, from costuming and local events to sex and role-playing games. Those who do come out to meet often consider themselves solitary and prefer to remain so. Covens exist in rural Minnesota but according to at least one member of the "old guard," an original Pagan community dating back to the 1960s, these covens are closed—preferring a similarity of age and ideology to eclecticism and what they see, somewhat justifiably, as a haphazard randomness cropping up in the new generation. The only evidence attesting to this old guard is the surprisingly rich occult section at the state university in Mankato. According to library employees, the section is heavily donation-driven.

Younger Pagans meet and socialize in off-beat venues like the Coffee Hag on Riverfront, but once finished with their schooling in Mankato they usually move on to find teachers outside this small southern Minnesota community. On occasion these Pagans work magic together, but more often than not they drift off to perform rituals on their own, carving their own path based on reading and any formal instruction they may or may not obtain. The weather and the needs of the homeland dictate the choices and commitments of these Pagans.

From Rural to Urban

On this night, at least seventy-five people pack the church rented by the local chapter of Covenant of the Goddess. They crowd around the circle—those in need of chairs sitting, the rest standing, all holding high candles for the Imbolc ritual. Outside the ceremony, the gravel parking lot just off of Lake Street in Minneapolis is filled with cars, many plastered with bumper stickers: "The Goddess Is Alive and Magic Is Afoot," "Wiccan Army," "Have You Runed Your Day Yet?" At the end of the ceremony, the circle splits apart as people join the feast, talking about other events taking place around the Twin Cities as the season opens.

In Minneapolis–St. Paul, all a Pagan needs to do to find community is to survey occult shops and coffee houses—where flyers cover the walls by the entry. Everything from public rituals to classes to "Pagan-friendly" business ads can be found here. You can pick just the right group to suit any spiritual or lifestyle needs, and with patience and persistence in chatting people up (hopefully without seeming too crazy) the door to the more organized Twin Cities Pagan community inches open.

There are Pagans in the Twin Cities area who have never needed to touch a computer to make contact with the city's Pagan community. While many of the younger generation still rely on the Internet for referral, much can be discovered by simply attending publicly advertised classes. Free publications such as *The Edge* float around the city, giving Pagans an overview of programs and lectures available in their own neighborhoods.

A few urban Pagans remain solitary, yet social—attending meetings at the University Pagan Society or simply running into those of like mind at a local nightclub. There are also plenty of opportunities for Pagans to meet one another at events specifically for the purpose. This includes the Pagan Meetup Groups on www.meetup.com and the Coffee Cauldron, a longstanding bimonthly meet and greet in St. Paul. Someone new to town can attend social events, workshops, classes, fundraisers, or simply haunt some the crossover subculture communities—such as the polyamorous, the leather-folks, or even historical re-enactment enthusiasts. Even the public libraries stock a quality assortment of books on the occult and witchcraft. There is in the Twin Cities a rich history of occultists and occult interest.

The Same But Different

The Internet has increased similarities between urban and rural Pagans. Now both sides of the spectrum can draw from a similar knowledge base stemming from their religious and personal experiences. All anyone anywhere need do is go to a computer, hop online, and post to a message board, mailing list, or website. While their experiences still differ in their day-to-day lives as Pagans, they have plenty of opportunity to compare and contrast experiences and to exchange materials, goods, and services through the rapid communication medium of the Internet.

A common discussion thread in Pagan communities highlights the disjunction between rural and urban life for Pagans. Namely, given enough time eventually Pagans will fall into talk about whether we are still an agrarian tradition when our world no longer operates on seasonal cycles. The question focuses on the premise that only those in rural areas feel the effects of the seasons and the cycles of change and are influenced in their daily lives influenced by the sow-reap cycle of farming and survival.

Any apartment-dwelling urban Pagan can assert that he or she very much feels the effects of seasonal changes: the freezing cold at bus stops, the tow truck on a snowy day acting as a harbinger of death, the relief at the first warm day of the season when people can walk outdoors freely, and the hot summer days of sidewalk cafes and strolls in the park.

Of course rural Pagans feel the seasons deeply, forced to dig snow to get to their doors and well aware of what a strong drought or too much rain can do to a farming community. Unfortunately, despite the best efforts of the Pagan Census website there are no accurate statistics about the proportions of urban to rural Pagans in the United States or elsewhere. To do so requires a demographic study, and a demographic study requires willing participation and, to some extent, funding. Unless mainstream publishing marketers demonstrate more interest in Pagans beyond the youth market, it remains unlikely that any study supplying definitive comparisons will appear anytime soon. However, based on common anecdotes and encounters, the operative assumption of this article is that rural Pagans and urban Pagans differ from each other greatly. This includes buying patterns and other social behaviors, these differences being

based as much on local culture as upon location.

Above all, rural Pagans do not enjoy the easy anonymity of urban life. Consequently, more rural Pagans mention that they attend mainstream churches as a way of maintaining social contact with their communities. Rural Pagans are much more likely to practice in secret, often keeping their religion from their families. The risks of discovery is seen as greater, and not entirely without reason. Employers can insist upon knowing the religious orientation of their staff with far fewer consequences in a small town than in a larger city where more jobs and more legal resources are available.

In contrast, Pagan Pride Twin Cities draws visitors from the Twin Cities and beyond. There are Pagans from as far afield as North Dakota and Iowa who attend this single festival every year in early fall. Although they design it to draw press attention, the coordinators scramble to make sure the interests of visitors are protected. A camera policy is established to ensure that people wearing ribbons do not appear in photos. Most of the coordination staff is local to the city. On the day of the event, it is almost entirely those from outside the Twin Cities who wear the ribbons, even as they claim they travel this far from home so they can attend an event where they stay unknown.

Beyond the conflict of the anonymous versus the public Pagan life, rural Pagans also still rely more on the Internet and must travel farther or make greater efforts to obtain supplies. New Age and metaphysical shops are slowly becoming more common in smaller towns; however, as evidenced by periodic news reports, some rural areas have neighbors that may not feel so neighborly towards such enterprises. Every few months the *Witches' Voice* reports news coverage on the establishment or demise of a Pagan-directed shop in a small community. Nearly all of the demises are colored by some group protesting something about the shop, and usually the focus on the religion of the owner. When metaphysical shops do open in smaller towns, owners feel compelled by such attitudes to take a more universally religious approach.

For instance, a glass case in a Hammond, Indiana store boasted a rich variety of athames and gemstone jewelry. Right next to the stand boasting pentacles, ankhs, and runes, there stood a "What Would Jesus Do" bracelet supply. Venturing further into the shop, saints' prayer books stood next to Florida water, and the book browser could pick up three versions of the Holy Bible as well as a basic book on spellcasting.

The gift shop in Amboy, Minnesota, greets the new customer with a room full of antique furniture and unique gifts. Only the persistent and informed will make it all the way to the back room, where there are drawers filled with herbs of every species and variety. The owners wait on a new customer, friendly but cautious—only when the name of a mutual acquaintance is dropped do they expand to mention a drum circle they run and to talk quietly of the celebrations and experiences embraced by their practices. The visitor is invited to attend, but is also cautioned not to come in next week and ask about it—the mother of one of the owners is visiting and helping with the shop; she does not know of her daughter's Pagan activities.

Occult shop owners in large cities enjoy the freedom to specialize. One shop can serve the Pagan/Wiccan community, another the Eastern-interest community (Buddhist, Hindu, and so on), and another can serve ceremonial magicians as a large city population supports all these shops successfully for several years. Their target market feels free to come out, purchase their goods, and network around these stores freely. After all, if a person runs into the boss at such a shop, the boss better explain what he or she is doing there, too.

Rural Pagans still fight harder to keep their secrets and to live freely as part of their greater communities. Urban Pagans are given a community of their own that can separate them from the greater part of a city. Oddly, as a result, in some ways the urban Pagans are more insular and less tolerant, as they can more easily choose with whom they interact.

While surface differences between urban and rural Pagans are falling away thanks to the Internet, the day-to-day questions on either side of the city limits remain the same: who to know, where to go, and, above all, how to practice. Despite valid arguments that say otherwise, these Pagans are all exposed to the will of nature and ultimately share a common bond according to the intent of their spirits. While those who live in cities think, act, and express differently from those who live closer to the land, there is a grounding in common as Pagans all find some way to tap from the earth or to reach for the sky.

The Pagan Vision Quest

by Dallas Jennifer Cobb

Vision quests originated in aboriginal communities. It is the process of taking oneself out of the everyday world in order to focus on spiritual matters, questions, and guidance.

In many cultures, vision quests mark rites of passage. As a person moves into a new community role, the quest helps them to understand their new responsibilities. Ideally, the vision quest shows how they will protect and provide for their community. In many cultures, every person is vision quested at least once. It is considered an essential step in the journey of life, and undertaken at times of transition.

Traditionally, vision quests were solitary retreats done in nature. Preceded by several months of social and psychological

Vision quests were a step in the journey of life, undertaken at times of transition, confusion, or uncertainty.

preparation, the quest would involve several days of sacred teaching, several days of solitude, fasting, and purification, and, after, a ritual celebration welcoming the new self back to the community.

While modern North American culture is more individualistic than our traditional cultures, we can still take the steps of social and psychological preparation, sacred learning, solitude, fasting, purification, and transition. While we may have to design and structure the ritual ourselves, we can still experience the transformational benefits of vision quests today.

Why Vision Quest?

In North America, many of us are disconnected from nature and alienated from our tribal roots. As a society we are groping spiritually and lacking a formal mechanism for focusing on spiritual matters, questions, and guidance. Inundated with technology, advertising, media images, and other noise, many of us never hear our inner voices, which are drowned out by all the clatter.

By reclaiming the tradition of vision quests, we can practice removing ourselves from the cacophony of everyday living and retreat to the calm of nature. Ideally we can reconnect with our spiritual selves and find our place in the greater web of life. A vision quest can be a powerful way to find a sense of purpose and identity. Extracting ourselves from the demands and distractions of our day-to-day lives, we can take time to ponder spiritual matters, and so receive guidance and healing.

At the same time our consumer culture urges us to appropriate other cultural traditions, taking ceremonies and rituals without permission or training. Please don't. While you may be tempted, this practice is cultural appropriation, and there is nothing spiritual about it. Take the time to find your own way to vision quest, to heal past wounds and examine your future paths. This article can help you to design a vision quest based on the spiritual principles of ancient cultural traditions, but shaped by you and reflective of your modern identity.

The Elements of a Vision Quest

A vision quest must be planned and prepared for. It is not something to enter into quickly nor lightly. It is good to choose a time that is significant for you in some way—a birthday, anniversary, or the date of a significant event.

Like any ritual, a vision quest must involve certain elements. Think about any ritual you have been part of. The format for that ritual can serve as a microcosmic template for a vision quest.

As in a smaller ritual, you will cast a circle, call in the directions, invoke the gods and goddesses you will be petitioning for help, raise the spiritual energy or power that is needed to work your transforming magic, ask your questions or state your intentions, be open to guidance, and listen and give thanks. When you have received the answers you came seeking, make an offering to the spirits that helped you, and then ground the energy you raised. Thank the gods and goddesses, and then purify and protect yourself as you prepare to leave the sacred space and return to the mundane world. Lastly, open the circle.

Creating Your Own Vision Quest Ritual

Using the general ritual format as a guideline, you can devise your own vision quest ritual. Meditate on your spiritual question or confusion, and concentrate on the aspect of your life that you want to change, understand, or seek guidance on. Let all your experiences play through your mind as you mull over the nature of the issue.

Obtain a notebook or journal which will become your vision quest book. Put all of your ideas, plans, and thoughts in it—recorded while planning the ritual, and afterward to record the revelations and visions of the ritual.

In the months before the quest, clarify your intentions. Write down what you are seeking. Write down the confusion or displacement you feel, and start to compose the difficult questions that have been plaguing you. As time passes you can add to, delete, and amend all of these. Ideally, you want to have one clear query—that draws your spiritual crisis in focus—to take with you.

Next, think about ways you can remove yourself from your everyday life and enjoy solitude and contemplation in nature. Only you will know what environments and surroundings evoke the spirit in you. While it is common to choose a quiet site in nature, this may not be practical or possible for all of us. So choose a site that will evoke some spiritual connection for you while keeping you safe and secure.

Once you have decided what you are seeking, and where you will go, start to plan and clarify the details of the ritual you will undertake. Talk it over with other like-minded people, especially those who have done vision quests themselves. Tell them what you are struggling with and talk to them about your spiritual crisis. Discuss what you are trying to create for yourself, tell them what you have in mind, and ask for their feedback. Make notes on what you are told and what is suggested. Be sure to call on these people for support when you are ready for the vision quest.

Spiritual Contemplation

Before you head out on your own, take the time to focus on your intentions and clarify what you seek. Asking specific questions about your intentions will help you to articulate and shape the nature of your quest.

Make lists of your strengths, gifts, and assets. Include your friends and allies, your passions and abilities, all the things that give you pleasure and power. This list will be a reminder of your greater good, something to call on during the vision quest should you need affirmation or support.

A list your fears and vulnerabilities is also useful. Made before you head out on your own, the list can help to prompt you to plan for things that might otherwise imperil you. If you are afraid of the dark and write this down, you will then remember to bring flashlight, or you will quest during the day. Our fears and vulnerabilities are only a danger to us if we succumb to them. To know your fears is to keep yourself somewhat safe from them through anticipation of, and preparation for, the very worst. Remember, better safe than sorry, and if you prepare for the worst, it rarely happens.

Make plans for safety and backup. Once you have determined location and time, call a few of your friends and tell them your plans. It is important to have one person who will be your primary backup. Tell this person precisely where you are going and what you plan to do. Let them be your safety support system, so that if you don't check in on time they can take the appropriate steps to find you. This person is a crucial safety net.

Carrying a cell phone in case of emergencies is a good idea. It allows you to call for assistance if your require it. Keep it charged and with you, but turn the ringer off. You don't want to be receiving any phone calls while you are trying to vision quest.

What to Take with You

Before heading out, you should consider carefully what you want to take with you on the vision quest. You may wish to take your journal and several pens to record your feelings, revelations, and new understandings. It is also advisable to take some power objects with you, such as ritual jewelry, sacred stones, protective herbs, or photographs of friends and allies. As you select what you will take remember two things: you have to be able to easily carry all this stuff, and these items should be uplifting and confidence inspiring. They will be icons of your strength, protection, and connection to your community.

You may wish to choose favorite or magical clothes to garb yourself in. The clothing can be imbued with magic and protective energy so that it aids you in drawing a circle of protection around your body. Depending on the season, a rain jacket or bug protection may become your magical garb.

Take sacred herbs if you choose to smudge and purify yourself, to offer to the Gods and Goddesses, or to ward off bad energy and keep you aligned with good magic. It may also be helpful to take a divination tool with you, such as tarot cards, scrying mirror, or pendulum. If you regularly use a divination tool, then take it and use it to tune in to spiritual guidance.

Often the gathering of protective items helps to plan the ritual in greater detail. These are reminders of a spiritual center, and so clarify what needs to be done. For many of us, this process also magnifies where we have strayed from our original intentions and helps us to understand some of the foggy areas we need to examine in our lifestyle, practices, and ways of being.

As ideas for the ritual occur to you, write them in your vision quest book so you can record the evolving process.

Into the Mystic

Solitude and quiet will help you hear the voices inside you, so a silent vision quest is recommended. Don't take any electronic gadgets or things that will overpower the voices within you.

While some people think fasting is an important part of vision questing, there is no hard-and-fast rule. It is said that fasting empties the body so that the soul may be fed. But feasting nourishes the soul and self-esteem. You will have to decide whether you need to fast or need to take sustaining foods with you. The choice is yours.

As you depart, ground yourself by declaring your intentions. Whether you state them aloud or write them on parchment paper, state your intentions clearly, identifying what spiritual matters you are seeking guidance on. Touch the earth, and know her steady energy goes with you as you journey and quest. Tell yourself that the earth will always be there to ground and steady you in times of uncertainty or fear.

Though you are entering further into a spiritual state, the mundane world will continue on. It is important to protect your body while you journey on the magical plain. Cast a circle of protection around yourself. Whether you smudge with sweet grass and sage or envision golden white light surrounding you, be focused and deliberate in protecting yourself. It is often advisable to do a vision quest on property owned by friends. This way, we can retreat to the solitude of the back woods but still enjoy the protection of allies nearby.

When you call in the directions, recount to yourself the elements of the directions that you will take with you as help on the quest. In your mind, add these elements to the circle of protection that surrounds you.

As you journey deeper into nature, let the journeying in the outside world be a metaphor for your journey into the inner world of spirit. As you explore the territory of your vision quest, journal the thoughts, ideas, and questions that occur to you. As random thoughts are written down they find a finite place in the world and can be linked with other seemingly random thoughts. Call on the gods and goddesses you have chosen to help you in the magical work you seek to do. Chant, sing, or meditate on your intentions so they are communicated to the deities that accompany you.

Chanting or singing combined with walking can raise physical and spiritual power, producing clarity within. As this energy flows, you will start to work your magic. Identify what you want to shed from your life and leave behind after the vision quest. Symbolically offer this energy up to the earth and to the gods and goddesses. If you have brought a symbol of this energy, leave it in nature and give thanks for the transformation of the energy out of your life. For ecology's sake, please choose symbols that are non-toxic and will decompose rapidly.

As you symbolically leave the vestiges of your former self behind, mindfully cleanse yourself of the past. Whether you choose a smudge of sweet grass or sage or a swim in a clear lake, be sure to focus on clearing and opening to the new.

When you have lightened yourself of what burdens you, ask for a sign, a symbol, or a vision. Open your senses to your surroundings, and feel the energy of spirit flowing all around. Your may find your vision in the trees, the sky, or in your thoughts.

When you receive your sign or vision, give thanks. Take some time to write. Put your thoughts, revelations, and feelings in your vision quest book, and give thanks to the gods and goddesses who have journeyed to be with you. Touch the earth and thank her for steadiness and support through your journey.

Returning to the Mundane World

Symbolically, a vision quest is a time of rebirth. You have chosen to leave the mundane world, and you reenter it augmented with the spiritual matter of the vision. You must consciously protect yourself as you prepare to return to the everyday world. You are changed and therefore vulnerable. It is advisable to make this transition slowly and gently, and to not enter into full-blown chaos right away.

As if returning from a vacation or traveling somewhere new, we possess new eyes and new perspective after our vision quests. Landscapes and vistas will be suddenly awe-inspiring; buildings and people will be fascinating and beautiful. With new eyes, we can be fully in the present moment and fully aware. We can leave our preoccupation with past and future aside, and we can be fully in the present moment

Whether journeying or in stillness, we can practice reflection, focus, and intention, weaving our new magic into the fabric of our lives. As we see things anew, we can practice gratitude for things we may have taken for granted, identify goodness in our lives, and amplify the good by focusing on it.

When we see the world anew with eyes of wonder, we remember a state of innocence and purity. This way, our everyday journeys take on a new meaning, becoming more spiritual in nature.

By making vision quests a regular part of our lives, we can reinvent ourselves according to our evolving ideas and desires, creating the spiritual satisfaction we seek in our lives. The vision quest can be used to make changes in our life path. After a vision quest we are new spiritual beings, better able to appreciate this great adventure of life.

The New Home of the Gods

by Steven Repko

In our searches for spiritual growth, we often forget that we do not live in the spirit world. Humans are physical entities, and spiritual accomplishment must be physically displayed to become "real" for us.

When I was young and lived in the middle of nowhere, I would muse for hours about the great circles that I would attend in an imaginary covenstead. I spent hours and hours finding the perfect Witch playground for making devotions to my gods and goddesses. Natural cedar groves, pristine pools, hidden rises, secret fields, and old forgotten sand quarries were among the places I frequented. I would envision processions, practitioners entering "there" and gathering "here." An imaginary altar in the north would capture the Moon's light,

empowering my rituals. Who cared back then if one would need a machete to get to my ritual sites for sabbat celebrations? I was a kid and my

Quite simply, humans have a hard time believing in something they can't see or touch.

thoughts were everything. Even then without knowing it I was formulating an anthropological observation.

In Pagan times past, temples both modest and luxurious were erected or adopted to create a sacred environment for the physical expression of spirituality. Quite simply, human beings have a hard time believing in something they can't see and touch. The temple concept provides a physical interface to the gods. It lets us touch them and helps us validate our religious belief in a tangible world.

We need divine purpose in our lives and also societal confirmation of our beliefs and practices. Physical sacred space provides a lovely opportunity to invite others to share our religious experiences and validate them through their participation.

What Is a Temple?

A temple is a planetary bookmark of the last place we publicly experienced a god, goddess, or other spiritual entity. In action, a temple inspires worship and communion with the divine. It can exist anywhere. The ancient Celts venerated spring waters or "wells" with modest fanfare. Water sustained life and was divine providence. It was a blessing from "our mother" to lessen our toil and ensure our health, well-being, and survival. Because the Celts could see and touch the water, they could see and touch the proof that the gods were involved in their lives. In time, they would often mark the spot so others could easily identify the sacred well and "worship" (drink and bathe) at this divine spot.

Men, women, and children do not live by water alone. Other cultures believed that an open or high place was closer and more

visible to the gods, and therefore a better place for them to observe worship. As time wore on, the industry of the faithful expanded the size and decor of their worship in an attempt to more closely reach toward the glory of the gods.

In their heyday the great Pagan societies erected major worshipping centers to their local gods and goddesses. Throughout the eastern world and Americas we see examples of the massive physical representations of spiritual veneration. These were and still are places where thousands of believers validate the reality of their relationships with deity. In the later days of Paganism and the early expansions of Judaism, Christianity, and Islam, many of these temples were either adopted outright or copied as the perfect example of what physical religious worship was supposed to look like. The bad news is our relationship to deity is not what it once was, and if you want a drink or a bath or you want to get closer to the gods you must go elsewhere.

Temples to the Various Gods

There were and still are fire gods, earth gods, water gods, and air gods, but thanks to modern inventions there are also money gods, health gods, parking gods, and of course the great mother goddess of soccer moms. All of these gods or goddesses can be served by temples in our modern spiritual world. They and our personal experiences of them can and should be commemorated for the inspiration of others.

Okay, so how do we create temples to suit all these gods?

Well, depending on your visual ideal the process can vary.

The modern method of temple building requires a large mortgage, thousand of patrons, and money to pay the electric and water bills.

Although the most recent examples of Pagan temples were rather impressively sized, the original temples were not usually behemoth. Instead, they were the size of roadside shrines in Nepal and those dedicated to the madonnas and saints in countries like Mexico and Poland. Generally, these are intimate and quiet (though public) places of public religious celebration and sharing. Both man-made and natural in their construction, they required no mortgage because they really didn't belong to anyone except the gods and goddesses. They simply were permanent sacred spaces on earth.

You could find them on the road from here to there and on any six square inches of a street corner. Temples, as you would expect, were a part of everyday life, and anywhere you found people you found temples.

In modern society, there still are "natural" placements of sacred inspiration. Many of them are encased in city, state, or federal forests—forever protected by our park and wildlife management systems. Additionally, modern man has erected numerous temples, shrines, and wells with his own hands in the forms of fountains, statues, gardens, arboretums, and other such monuments. Many of these commemorate divine vision or ideals that are easily adopted into our daily path-working, and if the statue is an undisclosed maiden or a Native American great father, all the better. Why adopt a highway when you can adopt a temple?

There is also nothing wrong with sharing the spiritual temples of other religious organizations. Every part of a modern church, temple, or mosque is compatible with Pagan worship. Bathe in all divinity and spirituality—there are no lines drawn; in deity, all are welcome.

With a little bit of tact, respect, and understanding, you will find the Paganism hidden in the symbols of all major religions. With a bit of effort, it will be quite simple to adopt the thousands of madonnas and novena chapels erected in the ancient memory of Isis and Artemis. These examples of perfect Pagan divinity stand today, so use them and embrace the energy of the historical divine.

Your Own Temple

Once you have chosen to build or adopt a temple, now all you have to do is worship. So go ahead, worship.

Worship, like deity, is in the eye of the beholder. You are solely responsible for constructing a system of worship for your temple. To do this you will need ask yourself some questions.

Is your temple dedicated to a particular god or goddess? What do they expect as worship? Do you leave offerings? If so, what kind? What worship needs will be particular to your god or goddess?

The inspiration of a temple is a personal thing. It can be shared, but it cannot be negotiated. You should seek to feel the true meaning of your temple and the divine purpose it contains. Ask yourself what are our benefits of worshipping here. Don't be afraid to ask "What's in it for me?" Too often we worship blindly without accepting responsibility for selecting both our deity and our method of venerating them. If you are not getting what you want from your gods, it's your fault.

Some final questions: When do you use your temple, and how often? If your gods expect offerings, what sort? Whether they are modest offerings or extravagant will affect the shape of your temple space.

Daily Miracles

When the gods are pleased, keep a record of what occurs. As with the ancient tribal and Wiccan mysteries, a record should be kept of the blessings bestowed at this site and imparted to others. After all, what good is a shrine if miracles don't happen there?

I am mystified daily by any religion that never stops to record any magic happening. We should be vocally proud and thankful of what the gods give us every day. Our temples should be built to mark stories of challenges thwarted and wonder imparted. We should have songs and stories of the modern grace of the gods, and the temple is where they should be performed.

Ready for Our Temples

Mythology and chronicles in place, offerings and holy days selected, customs and decorum within the temple committed to memory, responsibility in tow, we are now ready.

Allow me to impart some of my own chronicle with the hope of inspiring you to your own.

It was suggested in a dream by the goddess Hecate that I adopt a temple in a town center in order to venerate the spirit of a local "well maiden." An offering of fresh flowers was to be sacrificed in the "magical part of the year," and in return we would receive as our blessing the spirit of youth on the Full Moon, in the form of goddess water we could use in our magical workings. As the idea sounded simple enough, I proceeded with zeal.

On the first procession of my worship group at that location, we suddenly discovered something we didn't know. There was another goddess represented at the entrance to our "Maiden's Well" Temple. A corner Madonna stood to commemorate the blessings of Hecate who guided us to this spot. My guess is, she was bored and needed a little action of her own.

It would of course have been impolite to pass any goddess without leaving a gift in worship for her protection and guidance on our journey. In this way we expanded our mythology and our spiritual purpose, as we decided to reinstate the ancient offering custom of "leaving a cake" for Hecate. This was customary even after the conversion of Diana worshippers. We also left a monetary cash donation, as is customary in the Church we passed.

The spirit of the two goddesses working together has brought us serious and gifted younger dedicated members with unique spirits—great additions to our coven energy. Our 2004 Beltane Troupe was a direct result of the Maiden's blessings and Hecate's guidance in our spiritual purpose. In this way we have touched the entire local community, not just the Pagan one.

Temples in Daily Life

I make a point in my daily life of frequenting natural wells on a weekly basis, thus renewing my spirit and expanding sacred space as I expand my worship. Our mission as priests and priestesses is ever to expand sacred space and reconcile the physical world with deity.

Our coven has becoming quite adept at using public land for rituals and celebrations, and I recommend this highly. We have found that individually we actually have more rights to public land use than we would as an incorporated "church." Since we know that "every Witch is a religion," we now individually act as our own agents in dealing with public concerns. After all, a coven is not really an organization, it's an extended family. We are no longer regulated by governmental definitions that do not fit us—we are free to worship as the Goddess intended.

Perhaps that is the beauty in temple worship, that we have the freedom to commune with the gods and create sacred space in daily life. By working the divine into the mundane, we get to live in a blessed condition and inspire others to do the same.

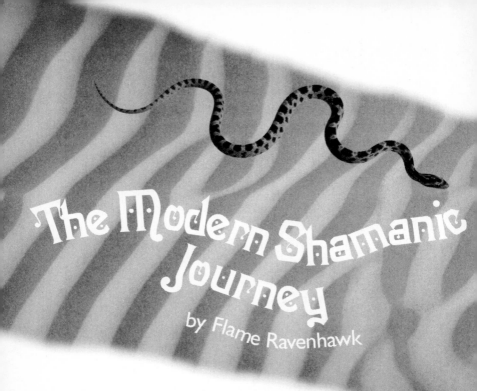

The Modern Shamanic Journey
by Flame Ravenhawk

Gerald Gardner's style of Wicca was influenced by a number of factors, including the folk traditions of Europe, Kabbalist philosophy, and ceremonial magic. Since then, Wicca has diversified even further with its expansion in North America. There are now many different ways that a Wiccan practice can be expressed.

Many people describe their tradition of Wicca as "shamanic" in nature, and some even refer to their practice specifically as "shamanic Wicca." But even formal Gardnerian Wicca has a shamanic history and core. The two terms are descriptions of practices that complement each other quite well. So what really do these modern practitioners mean by "shamanism"?

Shamanic Wicca Defined

In the broadest sweep of the definition, Shamanic Wicca is merely one way that the spiritual depth of Wicca may be expressed. It is Wiccan philosophy and practice melded with shamanic techniques and wisdom. It is not a "tradition" in that it is not a codified set of rituals that have been handed down in any one particular lineage. Rather, it's more of a general style of spirituality.

There are now many different ways that a Wiccan practice can be expressed.

So what does that really mean, anyway? What is shamanism, and how does it fit into a modern Wiccan spiritual context? Due to the large differences in interpretation of both shamanism and Wicca, these words can now mean almost anything to anybody. I offer a working definition as a practitioner of Shamanic Wicca for the past fifteen years or so.

Modern Wicca

Wicca is a religion that has, as many other world religions do, many different denominations. No one simple definition will suffice, and the very question of what makes one Wiccan is hotly disputed among both traditionalists and eclectic practitioners alike. However, Wicca has a fundamental aspect of expression, a very shamanistic aspect, that ties the various branches of Wicca together. Wicca is a flexible, modern spiritual tradition with very ancient roots.

Wicca, as defined by Gardner, is a "mystery tradition," meaning that a core aspect of the religion cannot be taught or explained, but must be experienced and revealed. It is fundamentally a religion of personal relationship to divinity. It allows individuals to connect with and express themselves as an aspect

of the divine. The same can be said of shamanic practices, which are also experienced rather than taught.

Wicca identifies deity as both masculine and feminine, and therefore honors both the God and Goddess. Wiccans believe in their ability to attune themselves to the energy of the universe. When they do so, they can direct the flow of this energy in order to effect changes in their lives. This is called magic, and the use of this energy is governed by the Wiccan Rede, which enjoins Wiccans to "harm none." Wiccans revere the Earth as their sacred home and follow a seasonal rhythm of celebrations called Sabbats. The Wiccan religion also includes a belief in an unseen spirit world, which is precisely where ancient shamanic practices enter in.

Technicians of Trance

Shamanism, although mostly thought of as a Native American phenomenon in the United States, is actually an anthropological term used to describe a specific type of spiritual practice. Shamanic practices can be seen in virtually every culture that believes in a spiritual "other world." Shamans generally act as intermediaries between the material and spiritual realms. The shaman travels to the world of spirit to gain wisdom and information, much like a Witch upon her broom. Shamanism seeks to link the practitioner to the spirit worlds, however they are conceived. These practices rely heavily on meditation, trance work, and other techniques of attaining different levels of awareness. As such, shamanic practitioners are sometimes called "technicians of trance." Traditional witchcraft is also historically familiar with this type of practice, in the form of recipes for "flying" potions and ointments. These vestiges of earlier shamanic practices are still present in modern witchcraft today.

Depending on the culture in which the shamanic practice has arisen, these trance techniques will take different forms. However, shamanism has a universal quality that allows this one term to encompass a wide variety of practices. It is this universal quality that melds so seamlessly into the Wiccan traditions. That is, in many traditional cultures the "shaman" and the "Witch doctor" were one and the same. They are identical practices whose roots stretch back through time.

In most fundamental aspects, shamanic practice is designed to cause a person's spirit to travel to deeper levels of reality in search of healing and wisdom, expressly to bring that wisdom and healing back into this world for personal and global benefit. For all of the benefits received by the shaman from the spiritual work, he or she is expected to return the service. "Shaman" is a job description of spiritual service to the community.

The Spirit Worlds

A shaman recognizes many more layers of reality than the one we commonly interact with. The world we live in, in all of its physical manifestations, is usually referred to as the "world of form" (or substance). Beyond the world of form are other layers (equally real yet intangible) called the world of spirit. A Shaman "travels" to these other worlds in many different ways, but most of them involve allowing the conscious mind to wander free of the physical body by means of trance or meditation.

A shaman may travel to the spirit worlds for many reasons. Some of these reasons include spirit healings (sometimes called "soul retrieval"), to gain information from the past, present, and future, and finally, to meet with spirit guides (or totems) to gain greater personal soul-wisdom.

In most shamanic traditions, there are three distinct spirit world realms: the world above, the middle world, and the world below. These designations are for general directional guidance only, indicating what direction the spirit may travel during a journey. They do not imply concepts of heaven or hell.

When the spirit of the shaman leaves his body, it may travel in three dimensions: up, down, or laterally. The three realms of the spirit worlds each encompass different qualities, and often operate in fundamentally different ways. Part of the Shaman's training involves exploring these realms and learning how to safely travel to them and through them.

If one chooses to go to the world above, it is to gain perspective on a situation. This is the realm of the akashic records, which store a memory of the entire history of the universe upon its ether. This is a very airy realm, filled with beings made from energy and light. In a place with few fixed landmarks; it is easy to get disoriented here, and is usually imperative to have an established relationship with a spirit guide before wandering too far in this direction. People who have spontaneous or unplanned "out-of-body" experiences generally drift in this upward direction, and the strangeness of the realm typically startles the wandering spirit right back into the world of form. However, with deliberate intent and practice, and perhaps an ethereal guide, one can learn to explore this realm at will.

A shaman travels to the middle world easiest by becoming very aware of the world around him. Focused attention on the physical world tunes the shamanic practitioner to this realm. This realm mirrors the mundane world, yet has a depth and complexity to it that is hard to describe. Imagine that the world as we know it is two-dimensional, like a photograph. Then imagine that a flat image from that photo expands and steps off the page. That's the kind of depth you find in the middle world.

Here everything has a visible aura, yet in most ways the forms duplicate the world we know. Matter is shown in its depth and complexity, and the intricate connections between all material things can be traced and followed. Travel or work in this world is commonly used for direct healing and various magical workings.

The world below is commonly the direction to go when searching for a spirit guide. This realm is both very solid in appearance and yet very changeable. It is filled with all of the things you might expect to see in the world of form, along with beings and places that are quite startling and unexpected. Colors, odors, and textures can seem much more distinct here, yet there's often a surreal quality to these, as well as a disjointed passage of time. There is a sense of the fantastical about this place—anything can happen, and at the merest thought.

This is usually where the shaman meets a spirit guides for lessons and sometimes even tests. This is also a good place to travel for soul retrieval, since fragments of a person's spirit often seem to get stuck in this realm. For this reason, healing energy for a person can also be found here. The world below is the playground of the spirit's imagination, as well as the proving ground for the soul.

Introduce yourself kindly and request a guide when entering this world for the first time. Although shamanic techniques are often best learned through direct instruction by one who has also explored these same paths, much of the training of a shaman happens through direct experience and with the personal guidance of the spirit beings who dwell in these realms.

As with Wicca, becoming a shaman often happens as a result of some form of initiatory experience. However, shamanic journey experiences sometimes happen to people without training or any other preparation. This is often caused by the spirit guides themselves stepping in to see that the person gets the instruction they need. These spontaneous shamanic initiations can be intimidating or disorienting at first, but with a trusting spirit, the person will receive the guidance he or she needs.

The Sacred Dreamer

In most cultures, a person is "summoned" to be a shaman. Either they feel an inner compulsion toward this style of practice, or some startling, life-changing event indicates this path. In some settings, the shaman position is inherited, with the secret knowledge and maps of the spirit realms handed down within families or similar small groups of practitioners. In some settings, a shaman chooses his or her likely successor and invests the time to train this person in the Spirit trails. But even careful training is not a guarantee of making a shaman.

Shaman is a very specific title that is not typically earned lightly. Some sort of extreme experience, often a life-or-death situation, traditionally creates a shaman. In some cultures, it is a deliberate, harsh initiation rite that proves the worth of a prospective shaman. In other cases, survival of a deadly accident can be seen as proof of the survivor's new role. The spirit worlds themselves will sometimes put a shamanic student through a crisis to test his or her worthiness. However it happens, the spiritual traveler "dies" in some form and is reborn as shaman. This same concept of a transformative death experience is found in many Wiccan initiations as well.

Being a shaman requires dedication and commitment, because it isn't easy. It is a role of selfless service to the community. A shaman, like a priest or priestess, will often serve many spiritually significant roles within the community. After all, he is the intermediator between the world of form and the world of spirit. He informs the community when relations between the two are out of balance by returning with messages from beyond the veil that separates them. He might also return with suggestions for what can be done to remedy this division. As such, the shaman is also a "sacred dreamer," envisioning a better future for the community and helping to bring this future to pass.

In many traditional societies, the shaman is also a healer, making no distinctions between physical and spiritual disease. When disease strikes a member of the community, the shaman may travel to the spirit worlds for the solution to the illness. Disease is thought to be an affliction of the soul, and it can cause pieces of a person's spirit to fragment, manifesting as illness in the world of form. The shaman cures this fragmented spirit in a process often referred to as "soul retrieval."

Shamanic techniques are designed to alter the consciousness in order to interact with the spirit worlds. Shamans specialize in the trance state. There are as many different ways to do this as there are cultures that support shamans. Drumming, dancing, meditation, sensory deprivation, fasting, psychoactive compounds, or a combination of these methods can be used to achieve shamanic trance. Temporal lobe epilepsy is also thought to be responsible for some historical cases of shamanic trance. Lucid dreaming and deliberate out-of-body experiences can also be considered a part of shamanic practice.

Shamanic Wicca

Many Neopagans and Wiccans use at least some shamanic techniques in their practice and rituals—especially the trance work done by way of guided meditations, sometimes called "pathworkings," within Wiccan traditions. However, practicing the techniques does not necessarily make one a shaman. You can blend shamanic techniques into a personal spiritual practice without being called to this specific service. When one is called to this path, the spirit worlds themselves usually find a way to make it known. Even so, because of the expanded awareness that can result from this style of work, it can enhance anyone's personal path, regardless of spiritual affinity or tradition.

So how do ancient shamanic techniques fit into modern Wiccan practice? Nicely, in fact. Shamanic techniques encompass a variety of ancient practices that still have relevance in the world today. With no dogma of their own attached, they blend seamlessly into the modern form and structure of Wicca and Neopagan philosophies and practices. May your own explorations of the spirit trails be filled with wonder and newfound knowledge. Enjoy the journey.

Pagan Travel Tips

by Ruby Lavender

Wiccans and Neopagans often enjoy travel because it allows them to indulge their curiosity about people, culture, and ideas. We also love to view nature, and what better way to experience the wonders of Mother Nature than to see its many facets in different parts of the world?

But some Pagans do not enjoy the nitty-gritty of traveling: the planning, the unexpected expenses, and the loss of authenticity that can come with prepackaged tours.

I am not going to recommend one mode of travel over another, as many people are simply more comfortable with

different ways of travel. But it is not hard to create your own unique itinerary, and it's also a great way to save money on some of those pricey package deals.

Speaking of Saving Money

I am going to recommend a non-Pagan resource: the *Let's Go* budget travel guides. These are compiled and revised every year by Harvard students, and are designed to offer basic information for tourists and to describe the most cost-effective ways to find lodging, food, and other needful things when traveling in most foreign countries. I have found them immensely helpful and usually carry one with me, heavily highlighted and dog-eared, on any trip.

Before you embark on planning your journey, ask yourself what sort of experience you want to have. Is freedom and flexibility important to you? Then you'll want to do your own planning. Do you want to enjoy the places and people and not have to worry about booking hotels or transportation? Then a travel agency is the way to go.

Fortunately, there are also a number of companies that offer trips which are ideal for Pagan sensibilities, including Earthwise Journeys (which promotes ecologically and socially-responsible trips) and

> Some Pagans do not enjoy the nitty-gritty of traveling: the planning, the expense, the prepackaged tours.

Footloose Forays (which leads trips into both exotic and mundane locales to discover the wonders of wildlife).

Some companies organize retreats for women to specific locales. If you do an Internet search for "Pagan travel" you will find loads of resources. Whether you want to go on a retreat, a group tour, a pilgrimage, or a solitary walking trip, you'll be sure to find some helpful information.

Where to Go?

Anyplace can appeal to Pagans; it's all in what you make of it. New York City can be a fascinating and spiritually rewarding place if you put your mind to it. On the other hand, the "ideal" trip to Stonehenge could end up being miserable if you plan things poorly.

The key is to be realistic about what you want to do, what you can afford to spend, and what sorts of potential problems might come up. For example, if you want to go hiking in Scotland, be aware that a few hours of wet, cold weather could drive you indoors for the remainder of your trip if you are not properly dressed. If you decide to visit markets in Nepal, do all you can to find out about local customs and etiquette so you can make the most of your souvenir shopping. If you want to see the pyramids in Egypt, be aware that travel in some parts of the world is sometimes suddenly restricted due to military conflicts.

Once you decide on the destination for your trip, you want to find the best way to get there.

How to Go?

If you're not planning to travel within your own country, chances are pretty good you're going to be getting on a plane. Maybe it's been a few years since you've flown—maybe you never have. You need to be aware that things are different these days, since the terrorist attacks of September 11, 2001. Airport security is much tighter and check-in takes much longer. International flights are especially rigorous in this regard, so plan to arrive for check-in at least two hours before your scheduled departure time.

Other modes of transportation are increasingly subject to security searches (especially following the train bombings in Madrid in 2004). This includes trains and buses. Be prepared for this, and don't carry anything illegal or likely to raise eyebrows.

If you are planning to rent a car once you reach your destination, make sure you get clear directions on how to reach the rental place from the airport. Also be aware that getting used to local driving customs may be stressful. Consider using local public transportation—it's a great way to immerse yourself in local communities, and you aren't going to have to worry about whether you're going too fast or too slow when that guy in the car next to you shakes an angry fist in your direction.

Where you stay will certainly affect your trip. Do you want to stay in the city center? That may be more expensive, but far more convenient. Do you want a rustic B&B? Be sure to book ahead of time as these can fill up quickly (summer solstice week is very busy in England, for example). Find out what meals are included, if any, and if your inn or hotel or hostel is near enough to shops, food, and the like. Hostels are fun but some can be a bit dicey, especially for women traveling alone. Some travelers feel more secure staying in a B&B—if you look around and compare prices, this can be a very affordable option.

If you plan to do some hiking, be sure to get some good maps, either before you leave or in situ once you arrive. Do remember that kilometers and miles are not the same thing at all. Don't try to do a day of strenuous hiking unless you are already an avid walker—getting in shape to do this by walking long distances for a few weeks before your trip is a good idea. Make sure you check the weather forecast before you head out. If traveling in a rural or remote area, it's not a bad idea to let your hosts know your plans for the day. They may be able to offer you some practical advice for getting around, where to eat, and so on.

What to Bring?

I know you're just dying to wear your colorful batik sarong or black velvet cloak on the plane. But don't. Don't make things difficult for yourself. Wearing loads of silver jewelry or steel-toed boots will just set off metal detectors. In fact, leave most of your jewelry at home; this way you sail through security checkpoints and reduce the risk of having it lost or stolen. And while you're at it, leave your athames and ritual gear at home too. It's just not worth it. Knives of any kind will be confiscated if they're not in your checked (as opposed to carry-on) baggage, but even if you think you'll be okay if you check them, don't risk it.

Speaking of carry-on luggage, you don't know misery until you've traveled with way too much luggage. If your trip is relatively short (a week or so), do yourself a favor and pack light. I personally do not like to carry more than I can comfortably carry while walking at a brisk pace. Those suitcases and bags with the little wheels for rolling may not work so well on cobblestones or sand or mud in far-off places. Get a solid duffel with sturdy zippers, and be sure not to pack all your valuables in the same bag in case your luggage is lost. Put a change of clothing and basic toiletries in your carry-on just in case you get stranded without your luggage.

As for clothes, you won't be happy you brought those sexy leather leggings once you realize how heavy they are to carry. You're traveling—most people won't get a chance to notice if you wear the same thing every day, so pack efficiently. Silk provides warmth as a layer in cold weather and also is lightweight for hot

156

weather—plus it washes and dries quickly. Bring at least one lightweight wool item in case it rains so you don't get cold and wet. Bring at least one change of shoes, too—sturdy sandals (like Birkenstocks or Tevas) with socks are a good bet because they're lightweight and comfortable. Jeans are not all that practical as they're heavy, but if you'll truly wear them every day, then go for it. I know I made fun of you for wanting to bring a cloak, but I have to say, when I was backpacking and sleeping outdoors in England, my wool cloak came in very handy to spread on the damp ground or use as an added blanket at night. Bring a scarf or lightweight vest to jazz up an outfit you'll be wearing often. Oh, and if you bring everything of the same color family, or simple neutral colors, you won't struggle with what to wear each day: black goes with everything.

What about other little things you may want to bring? Like candles. Or crystals. Or tarot cards. Here I will take a page from *The Accidental Tourist* and suggest that, if you would be very sad if you lost it, leave it at home. Matches and lighters are no longer allowed on planes, so candles might be suspect too. Besides, local innkeepers might not appreciate your lighting them in your room at night, no matter how careful you are. You and I both know you can perform rituals without any tools whatsoever. When traveling, it's really best to leave these things at home.

One thing I do recommend bringing, though: some essential oils. Lavender can be very useful for calming your nerves and helping you get to sleep when you're plagued by jet lag. Peppermint is good for headaches, fatigue, and nausea. Put the oils in small bottles and cap them tightly. And throw in some herbal tea bags while you're at it. Mint and chamomile both help settle the stomach, and chamomile helps you sleep.

What to Do

Do you like organized magical activities, or are you more of a solitary? Consider what you'd like to do on your journey to make it significant and meaningful for you. I have been to public rituals in London, Glastonbury, and at Stonehenge, but also have spent some magical time alone at sacred sites. You could try looking online for Pagan networking in the country of your destination. The U.K. and Australia have loads of sites listed, and many groups are open to having the public attend their events.

Another thought: If you behave as if you're moving to this city, you'll need to find the regular locales and shops for your Pagan-oriented life. Is there an occult bookshop? A vegan restaurant? An open-air theatre? A museum that has a substantial pre-Raphaelite collection? Where can you buy medicinal herbs? While you're looking around to experience what a new place has to offer, don't forget to seek out things specific to that place.

Perhaps you'd like to forge a magical connection with a certain spot by performing ritual or magic there. This is understandable. However, bear in mind that it is not usually appropriate to leave anything behind in a pubic place, spiritual mecca or not. For example, at sacred sites in the British Isles there is a lot of concern these days over "ritual litter." Pagan "pilgrims" bring crystals or other objects to bury near a site or place in the cracks of standing stones. But these objects lead to erosion.

Burning candles can leave wax behind which can alter the composition of ancient rocks or attract animals to an area unsafe for them. Even something seemingly innocent, like leaving a bundle of wildflowers inside a long barrow as an offering, is damaging: the chemical reaction that occurs when the flowers decay causes erosion of the rock walls inside the barrow.

I suggest you always follow the advice of the Ancient Sacred Landscapes Network (ASLaN): "Don't change the site; let the site change you." Experience a place's beauty and power for its own sake, carrying this memory within you without leaving anything of yourself behind.

Almanac Section

spring 2005 – spring 2006

The days & the nights, the
Moon & the stars, the colors
& the energies, & all the latest
Wiccan/Pagan news—the yearly
almanac gives you everything you
need to get you through this
heady astrological year

With news items written by S. Tifulcrum and Norman Shoaf

What's Listed in the Almanac
(and How to Use It)

In these listings you will find the date, lunar phase, Moon sign, color, and magical influence for the day.

The Day

Each day is ruled by a planet that possesses specific magical influences:

Monday (Moon): Peace, sleep, healing, compassion, friends, psychic awareness, purification, and fertility.

Tuesday (Mars): Passion, sex, courage, aggression, and protection.

Wednesday (Mercury): The conscious mind, study, travel, divination, and wisdom.

Thursday (Jupiter): Expansion, money, prosperity, and generosity.

Friday (Venus): Love, friendship, reconciliation, and beauty.

Saturday (Saturn): Longevity, exorcism, endings, homes, and houses.

Sunday (Sun): Healing, spirituality, success, strength, and protection.

The Lunar Phase

The lunar phase is important in determining the best times for magic.

The Waxing Moon (from the New Moon to the Full) is the ideal time for magic to draw things toward you.

The Full Moon is the time of greatest power.

The Waning Moon (from the Full Moon to the New) is a time for study, meditation, and little magical work (except magic designed to banish harmful energies).

The Moon's Sign

The Moon continuously "moves" through the zodiac, from Aries to Pisces. Each sign possesses its own significance:

Aries: Good for initiating things, but lacks staying power and quickly passes. People tend to be argumentative and assertive.

Taurus: Things begun now are lasting, tend to increase in value, and are hard to alter. Appreciation for beauty and sensory experience.

Gemini: Things begun now are easily changed by outside influence. Time for shortcuts, communication, games, and fun.

Cancer: Stimulates emotional rapport between people. Pinpoints need, supports growth and nurturance. Tends to domestic concerns.

Leo: Draws emphasis to the self, to central ideas or institutions, away from connections with others and emotional needs. People tend to be melodramatic.

Virgo: Favors accomplishment of details and commands from higher up. Focuses on health, hygiene, and daily schedules.

Libra: Favors cooperation, social activities, beautification of surroundings, balance, and partnership.

Scorpio: Increases awareness of psychic power. Precipitates psychic crises and ends connections thoroughly. People tend to brood and become secretive.

Sagittarius: Encourages flights of imagination and confidence. This is an adventurous, philosophical, and athletic Moon sign. Favors expansion and growth.

Capricorn: Develops strong structure. Focus on traditions, responsibilities, and obligations. A good time to set boundaries and rules.

Aquarius: Rebellious energy. Time to break habits and make abrupt change. Personal freedom and individuality is the focus.

Pisces: The focus is on dreaming, nostalgia, intuition, and psychic impressions. A good time for spiritual or philanthropic activities.

Color and Incense

The colors for the day are based on information from *Personal Alchemy* by Amber Wolfe, and relate to the planet that rules each day. This information can be taken into consideration along with other factors when blending magic into mundane life.

Time Changes

The times and dates of astrological phenomena in this almanac are based on Eastern Standard Time (EST) and Eastern Daylight Saving Time (EDT). If you live outside the Eastern Time Zone, or in a place that does not use Daylight Saving Time, adjust your times:

Central Standard Time: Subtract one hour.

Mountain Standard Time: Subtract two hours.

Pacific Standard Time: Subtract three hours.

Alaska/Hawaii: Subtract five hours.

Areas that have no Daylight Saving Time: Subtract an extra hour from the time given. Daylight Saving Time runs from April 3, 2005 to October 30, 2005.

Key to Astrological Signs

Planets		Signs	
☉	Sun	♈	Aries
♃	Jupiter	♉	Taurus
☽	Moon	♊	Gemini
♄	Saturn	♋	Cancer
☿	Mercury	♌	Leo
♅	Uranus	♍	Virgo
♀	Venus	♎	Libra
♆	Neptune	♏	Scorpio
♂	Mars	♐	Sagittarius
♇	Pluto	♑	Capricorn
		♒	Aquarius
		♓	Pisces

Festivals and Holidays

Festivals are listed throughout the year. The exact dates of many of these ancient festivals are difficult to determine; prevailing data has been used.

2005–2006 Sabbats and Full Moons

March 20, 2005	Ostara (Spring Equinox)
March 25	Full Moon 3:58 pm
April 24	Full Moon 6:06 am
May 1	Beltane
May 23	Full Moon 4:18 pm
June 21	Litha (Summer Solstice)
June 22	Full Moon 12:14 am
July 21	Full Moon 7:00 am
August 1	Lammas
August 19	Full Moon 1:53 pm
September 17	Full Moon 10:01 pm
September 22	Mabon (Fall Equinox)
October 17	Full Moon 8:14 am
October 31	Samhain
November 15	Full Moon 7:58 pm
December 15	Full Moon 11:16 am
December 21	Yule (Winter Solstice)
January 14, 2006	Full Moon 4:48 am
February 2	Imbolc
February 12	Full Moon 11:44 pm
March 14	Full Moon 6:35 pm
March 20	Ostara (Spring Equinox)

March 2005
Spring Equinox · March 20

March 20

Ostara · Spring Equinox · Palm Sunday
Waxing Moon
Color: Amber

Moon Sign: Cancer
Moon Phase: Second Quarter
Sun enters Aries 7:33 am
Moon enters Leo 8:17 am

☽ March 21

Juarez Day (Mexican)
Waxing Moon
Color: Silver

Moon Sign: Leo
Moon Phase: Second Quarter

♂ March 22

Hilaria (Roman)
Waxing Moon
Color: White

Moon Sign: Leo
Moon Phase: Second Quarter
Moon enters Virgo 8:10 pm

☿ March 23

Pakistan Day
Waxing Moon
Color: Topaz

Moon Sign: Virgo
Moon Phase: Second Quarter

♃ March 24

Day of Blood (Roman)
Waxing Moon
Color: Crimson

Moon Sign: Virgo
Moon Phase: Second Quarter

♀ March 25

Good Friday · Purim
Waxing Moon
Color: White

Moon Sign: Virgo
Moon Phase: Full Moon 3:58 pm
Moon enters Libra 6:00 am

♄ March 26

Prince Kuhio Day (Hawaiian)
Waning Moon
Color: Indigo

Moon Sign: Libra
Moon Phase: Third Quarter

☉ March 27

Easter
Waning Moon
Color: Orange

Moon Sign: Libra
Moon Phase: Third Quarter
Moon enters Scorpio 1:29 pm

March 28

Oranges and Lemons Service (English)
Waning Moon
Color: Ivory

Moon Sign: Scorpio
Moon Phase: Third Quarter

March 29

St. Eustace's Day
Waning Moon
Color: Scarlet

Moon Sign: Scorpio
Moon Phase: Third Quarter
Moon enters Sagittarius 6:56 pm

March 30

Seward's Day (Alaskan)
Waning Moon
Color: Brown

Moon Sign: Sagittarius
Moon Phase: Third Quarter

March 31 ♃

The Borrowed Days (European)
Waning Moon
Color: White

Moon Sign: Sagittarius
Moon Phase: Third Quarter
Moon enters Capricorn 10:48 pm

News Item (All items by S. Tifulcrum unless indicated)

Newscasters to Predict News

A Los Angeles entertainment lawyer is shopping around his weekly thirty-minute "Ahead-Lines News" format to the TV networks. Frank Lunn's show will have the look and feel of a real news program, with business reports, sports, weather, and national news—before it happens. "Ahead-Lines News" will feature top psychics doing the reporting, and include psychic field correspondents reporting from where news is expected to happen. Lunn says an on-screen accuracy rating will be updated weekly. Despite his confidence in the show concept, Lunn is unable to predict when it might air.

April 2005

♀   ### April 1

April Fools' Day   Moon Sign: Capricorn
Waning Moon   Moon Phase: Fourth Quarter 7:50 pm
Color: Purple

♄   ### April 2

The Battle of Flowers (French)   Moon Sign: Capricorn
Waning Moon   Moon Phase: Fourth Quarter
Color: Gray

☉   ### April 3

Daylight Saving Time begins   Moon Sign: Capricorn
Waning Moon   Moon Phase: Fourth Quarter
Color: Amber   Moon enters Aquarius 1:31 am

April 4 ☽

Megalesia (Roman)
Waning Moon
Color: Silver

Moon Sign: Aquarius
Moon Phase: Fourth Quarter

April 5 ♂

Tomb-Sweeping Day (Chinese)
Waning Moon
Color: Red

Moon Sign: Aquarius
Moon Phase: Fourth Quarter
Moon enters Pisces 4:45 am

April 6 ☿

Chakri Day (Thai)
Waning Moon
Color: Yellow

Moon Sign: Pisces
Moon Phase: Fourth Quarter

April 7 ♃

Festival of Pure Brightness (Chinese)
Waning Moon
Color: Green

Moon Sign: Pisces
Moon Phase: Fourth Quarter
Moon enters Aries 7:28 am

April 8 ♀

Buddha's Birthday
Waning Moon
Color: Coral

Moon Sign: Aries
Moon Phase: New Moon 4:32 pm

April 9 ♄

Valour Day (Filipino)
Waxing Moon
Color: Blue

Moon Sign: Aries
Moon Phase: First Quarter
Moon enters Taurus 11:50 am

April 10 ☉

The Tenth of April (English)
Waxing Moon
Color: Orange

Moon Sign: Taurus
Moon Phase: First Quarter

☽ April 11

Heroes' Day (Costa Rican)
Waxing Moon
Color: Lavender

Moon Sign: Taurus
Moon Phase: First Quarter
Moon enters Gemini 6:55 pm

♂ April 12

Cerealia (Roman)
Waxing Moon
Color: White

Moon Sign: Gemini
Moon Phase: First Quarter

☿ April 13

Thai New Year
Waxing Moon
Color: Brown

Moon Sign: Gemini
Moon Phase: First Quarter

♃ April 14

Sanno Festival (Japanese)
Waxing Moon
Color: Crimson

Moon Sign: Gemini
Moon Phase: First Quarter
Moon enters Cancer 5:03 am

♀ April 15

Plowing Festival (Chinese)
Waxing Moon
Color: Pink

Moon Sign: Cancer
Moon Phase: First Quarter

♄ April 16

Zurich Spring Festival (Swiss)
Waxing Moon
Color: Indigo

Moon Sign: Cancer
Moon Phase: Second Quarter 10:37 am
Moon enters Leo 5:17 pm

☉ April 17

Yayoi Matsuri (Japanese)
Waxing Moon
Color: Yellow

Moon Sign: Leo
Moon Phase: Second Quarter

April 18 ☽

Flower Festival (Japanese)
Waxing Moon
Color: Gray

Moon Sign: Leo
Moon Phase: Second Quarter

April 19 ♂

Women's Celebration (Balinese)
Waxing Moon
Color: Scarlet

Moon Sign: Leo
Moon Phase: Second Quarter
Moon enters Virgo 5:27 am
Sun enters Taurus 7:37 am

April 20 ☿

Drum Festival (Japanese)
Waxing Moon
Color: White

Moon Sign: Virgo
Moon Phase: Second Quarter

April 21 ♃

Tiradentes Day (Brazilian)
Waxing Moon
Color: Purple

Moon Sign: Virgo
Moon Phase: Second Quarter
Moon enters Libra 3:27 pm

April 22 ♀

Earth Day
Waxing Moon
Color: Rose

Moon Sign: Libra
Moon Phase: Second Quarter

April 23 ♄

St. George's Day (English)
Waxing Moon
Color: Brown

Moon Sign: Libra
Moon Phase: Second Quarter
Moon enters Scorpio 10:25 pm

April 24 ☉

Passover begins
Waxing Moon
Color: Gold

Moon Sign: Scorpio
Moon Phase: Full Moon 6:06 am

April 25

Robigalia (Roman)
Waning Moon
Color: Ivory

Moon Sign: Scorpio
Moon Phase: Third Quarter

April 26

Arbor Day
Waning Moon
Color: Black

Moon Sign: Scorpio
Moon Phase: Third Quarter
Moon enters Sagittarius 2:46 am

April 27

Humabon's Conversion (Filipino)
Waning Moon
Color: Topaz

Moon Sign: Sagittarius
Moon Phase: Third Quarter

April 28

Floralia (Roman)
Waning Moon
Color: Turquoise

Moon Sign: Sagittarius
Moon Phase: Third Quarter
Moon enters Capricorn 5:33 am

April 29

Green Day (Japanese)
Waning Moon
Color: White

Moon Sign: Capricorn
Moon Phase: Third Quarter

April 30

Walpurgis Night · May Eve
Waning Moon
Color: Blue

Moon Sign: Capricorn
Moon Phase: Third Quarter
Moon enters Aquarius 7:54 am

Ireland = Atlantis?

According to a new theory by Swedish scientist Ulf Erlingsson, the legendary island of Atlantis was actually modern-day Ireland. The geographer measured Ireland's landmarks and geography, then compared them to the description of Atlantis written by Greek philosopher Plato in 360 BC. Ireland's measurements match Plato's, and Ireland is the only island of the fifty largest worldwide that has a plain in the middle—an Atlantean landmark. Erlingsson also believes that the myth of Atlantis originated from Dogger Bank, an isolated shoal just off the coast of England. The bank sank after being hit by a tidal wave around 6,100 BC. The probability that Plato would have known about Dogger Bank is around 99.98 percent, estimates Erlingsson. His book *Atlantis from a Geographer's Perspective: Mapping the Fairy Land* was released in September, 2004.

May 2005

May 1

Beltane · May Day
Waning Moon
Color: Orange

Moon Sign: Aquarius
Moon Phase: Fourth Quarter 2:24 am

Sunday

☽ May 2

Big Kite Flying (Japanese)
Waning Moon
Color: Gray

Moon Sign: Aquarius
Moon Phase: Fourth Quarter
Moon enters Pisces 10:43 am

♂ May 3

Holy Cross Day
Waning Moon
Color: Red

Moon Sign: Pisces
Moon Phase: Fourth Quarter

☿ May 4

Bona Dea (Roman)
Waning Moon
Color: Yellow

Moon Sign: Pisces
Moon Phase: Fourth Quarter
Moon enters Aries 2:36 pm

♃ May 5

Cinco de Mayo (Mexican)
Waning Moon
Color: Purple

Moon Sign: Aries
Moon Phase: Fourth Quarter

♀ May 6

Martyrs' Day (Lebanese)
Waning Moon
Color: Pink

Moon Sign: Aries
Moon Phase: Fourth Quarter
Moon enters Taurus 8:01 pm

♄ May 7

Pilgrimage of St. Nicholas (Italian)
Waning Moon
Color: Indigo

Moon Sign: Taurus
Moon Phase: Fourth Quarter

☉ May 8

Mother's Day
Waning Moon
Color: Yellow

Moon Sign: Taurus
Moon Phase: New Moon 4:45 am

May 9 ☽

Lemuria (Roman)
Waxing Moon
Color: Lavender

Moon Sign: Taurus
Moon Phase: First Quarter
Moon enters Gemini 3:29 am

May 10 ♂

First Day of Bird Week (Japanese)
Waxing Moon
Color: White

Moon Sign: Gemini
Moon Phase: First Quarter

May 11 ☿

Ukai Season Opens (Japanese)
Waxing Moon
Color: Brown

Moon Sign: Gemini
Moon Phase: First Quarter
Moon enters Cancer 1:20 pm

May 12 ♃

Florence Nightingale's Birthday
Waxing Moon
Color: Green

Moon Sign: Cancer
Moon Phase: First Quarter

May 13 ♀

Pilgrimage to Fatima (Portuguese)
Waxing Moon
Color: Rose

Moon Sign: Cancer
Moon Phase: First Quarter

May 14 ♄

Carabao Festival (Spanish)
Waxing Moon
Color: Gray

Moon Sign: Cancer
Moon Phase: First Quarter
Moon enters Leo 1:17 am

May 15 ☉

Festival of St. Dympna (Belgian)
Waxing Moon
Color: Gold

Moon Sign: Leo
Moon Phase: First Quarter

☽

May 16

St. Honoratus' Day
Waxing Moon
Color: White

Moon Sign: Leo
Moon Phase: Second Quarter 4:57 am
Moon enters Virgo 1:46 pm

♂

May 17

Norwegian Independence Day
Waxing Moon
Color: Black

Moon Sign: Virgo
Moon Phase: Second Quarter

☿

May 18

Las Piedras Day (Uruguayan)
Waxing Moon
Color: Topaz

Moon Sign: Virgo
Moon Phase: Second Quarter

♃

May 19

Pilgrimage to Treguier (French)
Waxing Moon
Color: Turquoise

Moon Sign: Virgo
Moon Phase: Second Quarter
Moon enters Libra 12:30 am

♀

May 20

Pardon of the Singers (British)
Waxing Moon
Color: Coral

Moon Sign: Libra
Moon Phase: Second Quarter
Sun enters Gemini 6:47 pm

♄

May 21

Victoria Day (Canadian)
Waxing Moon
Color: Blue

Moon Sign: Libra
Moon Phase: Second Quarter
Moon enters Scorpio 7:49 am

☉

May 22

Heroes' Day (Sri Lankan)
Waxing Moon
Color: Amber

Moon Sign: Scorpio
Moon Phase: Second Quarter

May 23 ☽

Tubilustrium (Roman)
Waxing Moon
Color: Silver

Moon Sign: Scorpio
Moon Phase: Full Moon 4:18 pm
Moon enters Sagittarius 11:38 am

May 24 ♂

Culture Day (Bulgarian)
Waning Moon
Color: Gray

Moon Sign: Sagittarius
Moon Phase: Third Quarter

May 25 ☿

Lady Godiva's Day
Waning Moon
Color: White

Moon Sign: Sagittarius
Moon Phase: Third Quarter
Moon enters Capricorn 1:11 pm

May 26 ♃

Pepys' Commemoration (English)
Waning Moon
Color: Crimson

Moon Sign: Capricorn
Moon Phase: Third Quarter

May 27 ♀

Saint Augustine of Canterbury's Day
Waning Moon
Color: Purple

Moon Sign: Capricorn
Moon Phase: Third Quarter
Moon enters Aquarius 2:10 pm

May 28 ♄

St. Germain's Day
Waning Moon
Color: Brown

Moon Sign: Aquarius
Moon Phase: Third Quarter

May 29 ☉

Royal Oak Day (English)
Waning Moon
Color: Orange

Moon Sign: Aquarius
Moon Phase: Third Quarter
Moon enters Pisces 4:09 pm

May 30

Memorial Day (observed)
Waning Moon
Color: Ivory

Moon Sign: Pisces
Moon Phase: Fourth Quarter 7:47 am

May 31

Flowers of May
Waning Moon
Color: Maroon

Moon Sign: Pisces
Moon Phase: Fourth Quarter
Moon enters Aries 8:07 pm

News Item by Norman Shoaf

Anti-Pagan Activist Goes to School

PALMDALE, Calif. Preschool nowadays must be a pretty rough time, judging by a presentation given to Head Start educators last June in a Palmdale school. During a talk on "Cults and Gangs," the Rev. Billy Pricer, a fundamentalist preacher and volunteer sheriff's chaplain, distributed a "Satanic Ritual Calendar" that listed days when pagans allegedly gather for grisly rituals including child rape, dismemberment, and murder. The calendar also illustrated symbols supposedly linking gangs with the occult—such as a Star of David, a Muslim crescent, and a Nazi swastika. Outraged audience members filed a complaint with the community's Human Relations Task Force, which brokered an uneasy truce between Pricer and local Pagans. Pricer in the past presided over the disruption of a Wiccan ceremony in neighboring Lancaster in 2002. "It's a vendetta," Pricer said of the latest complaint. "It's sour grapes about that thing a couple of years ago."

June 2005

June 1 ☿

National Day (Tunisian)
Waning Moon
Color: Yellow

Moon Sign: Aries
Moon Phase: Fourth Quarter

June 2 ♃

Rice Harvest Festival (Malaysian)
Waning Moon
Color: Turquoise

Moon Sign: Aries
Moon Phase: Fourth Quarter

June 3 ♀

Memorial to Broken Dolls (Japanese)
Waning Moon
Color: White

Moon Sign: Aries
Moon Phase: Fourth Quarter
Moon enters Taurus 2:20 am

June 4 ♄

Full Moon Day (Burmese)
Waning Moon
Color: Indigo

Moon Sign: Taurus
Moon Phase: Fourth Quarter

June 5 ☉

Constitution Day (Danish)
Waning Moon
Color: Orange

Moon Sign: Taurus
Moon Phase: Fourth Quarter
Moon enters Gemini 10:36 am

☽ **June 6**

Swedish Flag Day
Waning Moon
Color: Gray

Moon Sign: Gemini
Moon Phase: New Moon 5:55 pm

♂ **June 7**

St. Robert of Newminster's Day
Waxing Moon
Color: White

Moon Sign: Gemini
Moon Phase: First Quarter
Moon enters Cancer 8:46 pm

☿ **June 8**

St. Medard's Day (Belgian)
Waxing Moon
Color: Brown

Moon Sign: Cancer
Moon Phase: First Quarter

♃ **June 9**

Vestalia (Roman)
Waxing Moon
Color: Crimson

Moon Sign: Cancer
Moon Phase: First Quarter

♀ **June 10**

Time-Observance Day (Chinese)
Waxing Moon
Color: Pink

Moon Sign: Cancer
Moon Phase: First Quarter
Moon enters Leo 8:39 am

♄ **June 11**

Kamehameha Day (Hawaiian)
Waxing Moon
Color: Blue

Moon Sign: Leo
Moon Phase: First Quarter

☉ **June 12**

Independence Day (Filipino)
Waxing Moon
Color: Gold

Moon Sign: Leo
Moon Phase: First Quarter
Moon enters Virgo 9:22 pm

June 13 ☽

Shavuot
Waxing Moon
Color: Ivory

Moon Sign: Virgo
Moon Phase: First Quarter

June 14 ♂

Flag Day
Waxing Moon
Color: Black

Moon Sign: Virgo
Moon Phase: Second Quarter 9:22 pm

June 15 ☿

St. Vitus' Day Fires
Waxing Moon
Color: White

Moon Sign: Virgo
Moon Phase: Second Quarter
Moon enters Libra 8:59 am

June 16 ♃

Bloomsday (Irish)
Waxing Moon
Color: Green

Moon Sign: Libra
Moon Phase: Second Quarter

June 17 ♀

Bunker Hill Day
Waxing Moon
Color: Rose

Moon Sign: Libra
Moon Phase: Second Quarter
Moon enters Scorpio 5:23 pm

June 18 ♄

Independence Day (Egyptian)
Waxing Moon
Color: Gray

Moon Sign: Scorpio
Moon Phase: Second Quarter

June 19 ☉

Juneteenth · Father's Day · Pentecost
Waxing Moon
Color: Amber

Moon Sign: Scorpio
Moon Phase: Second Quarter
Moon enters Sagittarius 9:45 pm

☽ June 20

Flag Day (Argentinian)
Waxing Moon
Color: Silver

Moon Sign: Sagittarius
Moon Phase: Second Quarter

♂ June 21

Litha · Summer Solstice
Waxing Moon
Color: Gray

Moon Sign: Sagittarius
Moon Phase: Second Quarter
Moon enters Capricorn 10:52 pm
Sun enters Cancer 2:46 am

☿ June 22

Rose Festival (English)
Waxing Moon
Color: Topaz

Moon Sign: Capricorn
Moon Phase: Full Moon 12:14 am

♃ June 23

St. John's Eve
Waning Moon
Color: Crimson

Moon Sign: Capricorn
Moon Phase: Third Quarter
Moon enters Aquarius 10:36 pm

♀ June 24

St. John's Day
Waning Moon
Color: Purple

Moon Sign: Aquarius
Moon Phase: Third Quarter

♄ June 25

Fiesta of Santa Orosia (Spanish)
Waning Moon
Color: Brown

Moon Sign: Aquarius
Moon Phase: Third Quarter
Moon enters Pisces 11:03 pm

☉ June 26

Pied Piper Day (German)
Waning Moon
Color: Yellow

Moon Sign: Pisces
Moon Phase: Third Quarter

June 27 ☽

Day of the Seven Sleepers (Islamic)
Waning Moon
Color: Lavender

Moon Sign: Pisces
Moon Phase: Third Quarter

June 28 ♂

Paul Bunyan Day
Waning Moon
Color: Scarlet

Moon Sign: Pisces
Moon Phase: Third Quarter 2:23 pm
Moon enters Aries 1:51 am

June 29 ☿

St. Peter and St. Paul's Day
Waning Moon
Color: Brown

Moon Sign: Aries
Moon Phase: Fourth Quarter

June 30 ♃

The Burning of the Three Firs (French)
Waning Moon
Color: Purple

Moon Sign: Aries
Moon Phase: Fourth Quarter
Moon enters Taurus 7:45 am

News Item

Norwegian Witch Wins Government Grant

Thirty-three-year-old Lena Skarning of Norway has become the country's only "state-backed Witch." She was awarded a government grant worth 53,000 kroner, or approximately $7,500, to help set up her new business, Forest Witch Magic Consulting. The business will offer fortunetelling, corporate seminars on magic, and various potions and creams to cure common aliments. Though officials from the development fund awarding the grant said Skarning's business plan was "reasonable and well thought out," they did attach a condition. Skarning had to promise not to cast spells that might hurt someone.

July 2005

♀ July 1

Climbing Mount Fuji (Japanese)
Waning Moon
Color: Coral

Moon Sign: Taurus
Moon Phase: Fourth Quarter

♄ July 2

Heroes' Day (Zambian)
Waning Moon
Color: Gray

Moon Sign: Taurus
Moon Phase: Fourth Quarter
Moon enters Gemini 14:26 pm

☉ July 3

Indian Sun Dance (Native American)
Waning Moon
Color: Orange

Moon Sign: Gemini
Moon Phase: Fourth Quarter

July 4 ☽

Independence Day
Waning Moon
Color: White

Moon Sign: Gemini
Moon Phase: Fourth Quarter

July 5 ♂

Tynwald (Nordic)
Waning Moon
Color: Maroon

Moon Sign: Gemini
Moon Phase: Fourth Quarter
Moon enters Cancer 3:07 am

July 6 ☿

Khao Phansa Day (Thai)
Waning Moon
Color: Yellow

Moon Sign: Cancer
Moon Phase: New Moon 8:02 am

July 7 ♃

Weaver's Festival (Japanese)
Waxing Moon
Color: Green

Moon Sign: Cancer
Moon Phase: First Quarter
Moon enters Leo 3:11 pm

July 8 ♀

St. Elizabeth's Day (Portuguese)
Waxing Moon
Color: White

Moon Sign: Leo
Moon Phase: First Quarter

July 9 ♄

Battle of Sempach Day (Swiss)
Waxing Moon
Color: Indigo

Moon Sign: Leo
Moon Phase: First Quarter

July 10 ☉

Lady Godiva Day (English)
Waxing Moon
Color: Amber

Moon Sign: Leo
Moon Phase: First Quarter
Moon enters Virgo 3:57 am

☽ **July 11**

Revolution Day (Mongolian)
Waxing Moon
Color: Gray

Moon Sign: Virgo
Moon Phase: First Quarter

♂ **July 12**

Lobster Carnival (Nova Scotian)
Waxing Moon
Color: Red

Moon Sign: Virgo
Moon Phase: First Quarter
Moon enters Libra 4:09 pm

☿ **July 13**

Festival of the Three Cows (Spanish)
Waxing Moon
Color: Brown

Moon Sign: Libra
Moon Phase: First Quarter

♃ **July 14**

Bastille Day (French)
Waxing Moon
Color: Turquoise

Moon Sign: Libra
Moon Phase: Second Quarter 11:20 am

♀ **July 15**

St. Swithin's Day
Waxing Moon
Color: Pink

Moon Sign: Libra
Moon Phase: Second Quarter
Moon enters Scorpio 1:51 am

♄ **July 16**

Our Lady of Carmel
Waxing Moon
Color: Blue

Moon Sign: Scorpio
Moon Phase: Second Quarter

☉ **July 17**

Rivera Day (Puerto Rican)
Waxing Moon
Color: Yellow

Moon Sign: Scorpio
Moon Phase: Second Quarter
Moon enters Sagittarius 7:35 am

July 18 ☽

Gion Matsuri Festival (Japanese)
Waxing Moon
Color: Silver

Moon Sign: Sagittarius
Moon Phase: Second Quarter

July 19 ♂

Flitch Day (English)
Waxing Moon
Color: Black

Moon Sign: Sagittarius
Moon Phase: Second Quarter
Moon enters Capricorn 9:26 am

July 20 ☿

Binding of Wreaths (Lithuanian)
Waxing Moon
Color: White

Moon Sign: Capricorn
Moon Phase: Second Quarter

July 21 ♃

National Day (Belgian)
Waxing Moon
Color: Purple

Moon Sign: Capricorn
Moon Phase: Full Moon 7:00 am
Moon enters Aquarius 8:55 am

July 22 ♀

St. Mary Magdalene's Day
Waning Moon
Color: Rose

Moon Sign: Aquarius
Moon Phase: Third Quarter
Sun enters Leo 1:41 pm

July 23 ♄

Mysteries of Santa Cristina (Italian)
Waning Moon
Color: Brown

Moon Sign: Aquarius
Moon Phase: Third Quarter
Moon enters Pisces 8:12 am

July 24 ☉

Pioneer Day (Mormon)
Waning Moon
Color: Gold

Moon Sign: Pisces
Moon Phase: Third Quarter

July 25

St. James' Day
Waning Moon
Color: Ivory

Moon Sign: Pisces
Moon Phase: Third Quarter
Moon enters Aries 9:23 am

July 26

St. Anne's Day
Waning Moon
Color: White

Moon Sign: Aries
Moon Phase: Third Quarter

July 27

Sleepyhead Day (Finnish)
Waning Moon
Color: Topaz

Moon Sign: Aries
Moon Phase: Fourth Quarter 11:19 pm
Moon enters Taurus 1:54 pm

July 28

Independence Day (Peruvian)
Waning Moon
Color: Crimson

Moon Sign: Taurus
Moon Phase: Fourth Quarter

July 29

Pardon of the Birds (French)
Waning Moon
Color: Purple

Moon Sign: Taurus
Moon Phase: Fourth Quarter
Moon enters Gemini 10:02 pm

July 30

Micmac Festival of St. Ann
Waning Moon
Color: Black

Moon Sign: Gemini
Moon Phase: Fourth Quarter

July 31

Weighing of the Aga Khan (Ismaili Muslim)
Waning Moon
Color: Amber

Moon Sign: Gemini
Moon Phase: Fourth Quarter

Talking Tombstones

Inventor Robert Barrows filed a patent application for a tombstone equipped with a video system. If the application is approved, the California inventor hopes people will use his system to leave videos in their hollow tombstones. The tombstones will be powered by the cemetery's lighting system and feature a flat touch screen with a computer that employs either a microchip memory or hard disk to store the electronic message. Although another tombstone design already displays electronic photos, Barrow's tombstone will be the first to include contributions from the deceased.

News Item

Paraplegic Magician Drives Blindfolded across the United States

On June 30, 2004, paraplegic magician Jim Passe donned a blindfold and got behind the wheel of a car to begin a 3,000-mile cross-country journey from New York to Los Angeles. Passe hoped his trip would increase awareness of disability issues. The adventure, which ended safely in Los Angeles on July 6, left Passe with an eye infection and a urinary tract infection. Two assistants took photos of motorists' expressions upon seeing the blindfolded Passe driving. Despite the blindfold, the magician didn't have a single accident while driving. Passe said he said he did come close to having a fender-bender while driving in Manhattan.

August 2005

August 1

Lammas
Waning Moon
Color: Gray

Moon Sign: Gemini
Moon Phase: Fourth Quarter
Moon enters Cancer 8:52 am

August 2

♂

Porcingula (Native American)
Waning Moon
Color: Black

Moon Sign: Cancer
Moon Phase: Fourth Quarter

August 3

☿

Drimes (Greek)
Waning Moon
Color: Yellow

Moon Sign: Cancer
Moon Phase: Fourth Quarter
Moon enters Leo 9:10 pm

August 4

♃

Cook Islands Constitution Celebration
Waning Moon
Color: Green

Moon Sign: Leo
Moon Phase: New Moon 11:05 pm

August 5

♀

Benediction of the Sea (French)
Waxing Moon
Color: White

Moon Sign: Leo
Moon Phase: First Quarter

August 6

♄

Hiroshima Peace Ceremony
Waxing Moon
Color: Indigo

Moon Sign: Leo
Moon Phase: First Quarter
Moon enters Virgo 9:54 am

August 7

☉

Republic Day (Ivory Coast)
Waxing Moon
Color: Orange

Moon Sign: Virgo
Moon Phase: First Quarter

August 8 ☽

Dog Days (Japanese)
Waxing Moon
Color: Lavender

Moon Sign: Virgo
Moon Phase: First Quarter
Moon enters Libra 10:8 pm

August 9 ♂

Nagasaki Peace Ceremony
Waxing Moon
Color: Gray

Moon Sign: Libra
Moon Phase: First Quarter

August 10 ☿

St. Lawrence's Day
Waxing Moon
Color: Brown

Moon Sign: Libra
Moon Phase: First Quarter

August 11 ♃

Puck Fair (Irish)
Waxing Moon
Color: Purple

Moon Sign: Libra
Moon Phase: First Quarter
Moon enters Scorpio 8:25 am

August 12 ♀

Fiesta of Santa Clara
Waxing Moon
Color: Pink

Moon Sign: Scorpio
Moon Phase: Second Quarter 10:38 pm

August 13 ♄

Women's Day (Tunisian)
Waxing Moon
Color: Black

Moon Sign: Scorpio
Moon Phase: Second Quarter
Moon enters Sagittarius 3:47 pm

August 14 ☉

Festival at Sassari
Waxing Moon
Color: Amber

Moon Sign: Sagittarius
Moon Phase: Second Quarter

☽ **August 15**

Assumption Day

Moon Sign: Sagittarius

Waxing Moon

Moon Phase: Second Quarter

Color: Silver

Moon enters Capricorn 7:13 pm

♂ **August 16**

Festival of Minstrels (European)

Moon Sign: Capricorn

Waxing Moon

Moon Phase: Second Quarter

Color: Red

☿ **August 17**

Feast of the Hungry Ghosts (Chinese)

Moon Sign: Capricorn

Waxing Moon

Moon Phase: Second Quarter

Color: Topaz

Moon enters Aquarius 7:39 pm

♃ **August 18**

St. Helen's Day

Moon Sign: Aquarius

Waxing Moon

Moon Phase: Second Quarter

Color: Turquoise

♀ **August 19**

Rustic Vinalia (Roman)

Moon Sign: Aquarius

Waxing Moon

Moon Phase: Full Moon 1:53 pm

Color: Coral

Moon enters Pisces 6:52 pm

♄ **August 20**

Constitution Day (Hungarian)

Moon Sign: Pisces

Waning Moon

Moon Phase: Third Quarter

Color: Blue

☉ **August 21**

Consualia (Roman)

Moon Sign: Pisces

Waning Moon

Moon Phase: Third Quarter

Color: Yellow

Moon enters Aries 7:01 pm

August 22

Feast of the Queenship of Mary (English)
Waning Moon
Color: Ivory

Moon Sign: Aries
Moon Phase: Third Quarter
Sun enters Virgo 8:45 pm

August 23

National Day (Romanian)
Waning Moon
Color: Scarlet

Moon Sign: Aries
Moon Phase: Third Quarter
Moon enters Taurus 9:58 pm

August 24

St. Bartholomew's Day
Waning Moon
Color: White

Moon Sign: Taurus
Moon Phase: Third Quarter

August 25

Feast of the Green Corn (Native American)
Waning Moon
Color: Crimson

Moon Sign: Taurus
Moon Phase: Third Quarter

August 26

Pardon of the Sea (French)
Waning Moon
Color: Rose

Moon Sign: Taurus
Moon Phase: Fourth Quarter 11:18 am
Moon enters Gemini 4:43 am

August 27

Summer Break (English)
Waning Moon
Color: Brown

Moon Sign: Gemini
Moon Phase: Fourth Quarter

August 28 ☉

St. Augustine's Day
Waning Moon
Color: Gold

Moon Sign: Gemini
Moon Phase: Fourth Quarter
Moon enters Cancer 2:57 pm

August 29

St. John's Beheading
Waning Moon
Color: Gray

Moon Sign: Cancer
Moon Phase: Fourth Quarter

August 30

St. Rose of Lima Day (Peruvian)
Waning Moon
Color: Maroon

Moon Sign: Cancer
Moon Phase: Fourth Quarter

August 31

Unto These Hills Pageant (Cherokee)
Waning Moon
Color: Brown

Moon Sign: Cancer
Moon Phase: Fourth Quarter
Moon enters Leo 3:14 am

News Item

Osbourne Family Seeks Revenge

Simon Cowell, a judge for the televised singing competitions *American Idol* in the U.S. and *Pop Idol* in the U.K., never hesitates to express his opinion. When rocker Ozzy Osbourne had a bad bike accident, Cowell opined that it was probably just a publicity stunt. Angered by Cowell's comment, the Osbourne family sought the aid of British white Witch Kevin Carlyon for revenge. Carlyon recruited hundreds of Scottish Witches to cast spells. One spell was to make Cowell lose his voice during the *Pop Idol* final. Another was to help Ozzy heal after the accident. A third spell was to keep Ozzy's single, recorded with daughter Kelly, at the top of the charts, and so block the various *Pop Idol* singles released over the winter holidays.

September 2005

September 1   ♃

Greek New Year

Waning Moon

Color: White

Moon Sign: Leo

Moon Phase: Fourth Quarter

September 2   ♀

St. Mamas' Day

Waning Moon

Color: Pink

Moon Sign: Leo

Moon Phase: Fourth Quarter

Moon enters Virgo 3:56 pm

September 3   ♄

Founder's Day (San Marino)

Waning Moon

Color: Black

Moon Sign: Virgo

Moon Phase: New Moon 2:45 pm

September 4

Los Angeles' Birthday

Waxing Moon

Color: Orange

Moon Sign: Virgo

Moon Phase: First Quarter

☽

September 5

Labor Day (observed)
Waxing Moon
Color: Lavender

Moon Sign: Virgo
Moon Phase: First Quarter
Moon enters Libra 3:52 am

♂

September 6

The Virgin of Remedies (Spanish)
Waxing Moon
Color: Red

Moon Sign: Libra
Moon Phase: First Quarter

☿

September 7

Festival of the Durga (Hindu)
Waxing Moon
Color: Yellow

Moon Sign: Libra
Moon Phase: First Quarter
Moon enters Scorpio 2:10 pm

♃

September 8

Birthday of the Virgin Mary
Waxing Moon
Color: Purple

Moon Sign: Scorpio
Moon Phase: First Quarter

♀

September 9

Chrysanthemum Festival (Japanese)
Waxing Moon
Color: Coral

Moon Sign: Scorpio
Moon Phase: First Quarter
Moon enters Sagittarius 10:03 pm

♄

September 10

Festival of the Poets (Japanese)
Waxing Moon
Color: Brown

Moon Sign: Sagittarius
Moon Phase: First Quarter

☉

September 11

Coptic New Year
Waxing Moon
Color: Yellow

Moon Sign: Sagittarius
Moon Phase: Second Quarter 7:37 am

September 12 ☽

National Day (Ethiopian)
Waxing Moon
Color: Gray

Moon Sign: Sagittarius
Moon Phase: Second Quarter
Moon enters Capricorn 2:56 am

September 13 ♂

The Gods' Banquet (Roman)
Waxing Moon
Color: Black

Moon Sign: Capricorn
Moon Phase: Second Quarter

September 14 ☿

Holy Cross Day
Waxing Moon
Color: White

Moon Sign: Capricorn
Moon Phase: Second Quarter
Moon enters Aquarius 5:02 am

September 15 ♃

Birthday of the Moon (Chinese)
Waxing Moon
Color: Turquoise

Moon Sign: Aquarius
Moon Phase: Second Quarter
Moon enters Pisces 5:24 am

September 16 ♀

Mexican Independence Day
Waxing Moon
Color: Rose

Moon Sign: Pisces
Moon Phase: Second Quarter

September 17 ♄

Von Steuben's Day
Waxing Moon
Color: Blue

Moon Sign: Pisces
Moon Phase: Full Moon 10:01 pm

September 18 ☉

Dr. Johnson's Birthday
Waning Moon
Color: Gold

Moon Sign: Pisces
Moon Phase: Third Quarter
Moon enters Aries 5:43 am

☽ **September 19**

St. Januarius' Day (Italian)
Waning Moon
Color: White

Moon Sign: Aries
Moon Phase: Third Quarter

♂ **September 20**

St. Eustace's Day
Waning Moon
Color: Maroon

Moon Sign: Aries
Moon Phase: Third Quarter
Moon enters Taurus 7:47 am

☿ **September 21**

Christ's Hospital Founder's Day (British)
Waning Moon
Color: Topaz

Moon Sign: Taurus
Moon Phase: Third Quarter

♃ **September 22**

Mabon · Fall Equinox
Waning Moon
Color: Green

Moon Sign: Taurus
Moon Phase: Third Quarter
Moon enters Gemini 1:07 pm
Sun enters Libra 6:23 pm

♀ **September 23**

Shubun no Hi (Chinese)
Waning Moon
Color: Purple

Moon Sign: Gemini
Moon Phase: Third Quarter

♄ **September 24**

Schwenkenfelder Thanksgiving (Germ.-American)
Waning Moon
Color: Indigo

Moon Sign: Gemini
Moon Phase: Third Quarter
Moon enters Cancer 10:10 pm

☉ **September 25**

Doll's Memorial Service (Japanese)
Waning Moon
Color: Amber

Moon Sign: Cancer
Moon Phase: Fourth Quarter 2:41 am

September 26

Feast of Santa Justina (Mexican)
Waning Moon
Color: Ivory

Moon Sign: Cancer
Moon Phase: Fourth Quarter

September 27

Saints Cosmas and Damian's Day
Waning Moon
Color: White

Moon Sign: Cancer
Moon Phase: Fourth Quarter
Moon enters Leo 10:03 am

September 28

Confucius' Birthday
Waning Moon
Color: Brown

Moon Sign: Leo
Moon Phase: Fourth Quarter

September 29

Michaelmas
Waning Moon
Color: Crimson

Moon Sign: Leo
Moon Phase: Fourth Quarter
Moon enters Virgo 10:44 pm

September 30

St. Jerome's Day
Waning Moon
Color: White

Moon Sign: Virgo
Moon Phase: Fourth Quarter

Badgers Threaten Stonehenge

Badgers living near Stonehenge are damaging various archaeological sites and ancient human remains around the protected monument. The animals are digging into prehistoric burial mounds and have already disturbed some of the remains and artifacts buried there. Though the Ministry of Defence has been trying to coax the badgers away to other locations, there has been little success. Officials will not consider culling the badgers. An archaeologist employed by the Ministry said some of the sites will have to be given up to the badgers, because the damage already is too extensive. Studies on the best methods to relocate the badgers continue.

October 2005

♄

October 1

Armed Forces Day (South Korean)
Waning Moon
Color: Gray

Moon Sign: Virgo
Moon Phase: Fourth Quarter

☉

October 2

Old Man's Day (Virgin Islands)
Waning Moon
Color: Yellow

Moon Sign: Virgo
Moon Phase: Fourth Quarter
Moon enters Libra 10:24 am

October 3

Moroccan New Year's Day

Waning Moon

Color: White

Moon Sign: Libra

Moon Phase: New Moon 6:28 am

October 4

Rosh Hashanah · Ramadan begins

Waxing Moon

Color: Red

Moon Sign: Libra

Moon Phase: First Quarter

Moon enters Scorpio 8:03 pm

October 5

Republic Day (Portuguese)

Waxing Moon

Color: Topaz

Moon Sign: Scorpio

Moon Phase: First Quarter

October 6

Dedication of the Virgin's Crowns (English)

Waning Moon

Color: Purple

Moon Sign: Scorpio

Moon Phase: First Quarter

October 7

Kermesse (German)

Waxing Moon

Color: Pink

Moon Sign: Scorpio

Moon Phase: First Quarter

Moon enters Sagittarius 3:28 am

October 8

Okunchi (Japanese)

Waxing Moon

Color: Black

Moon Sign: Sagittarius

Moon Phase: First Quarter

October 9

Alphabet Day (South Korean)

Waxing Moon

Color: Orange

Moon Sign: Sagittarius

Moon Phase: First Quarter

Moon enters Capricorn 8:43 am

☽ October 10

Columbus Day (observed)
Waxing Moon
Color: Lavender

Moon Sign: Capricorn
Moon Phase: Second Quarter 3:01 pm

♂ October 11

Meditrinalia (Roman)
Waxing Moon
Color: White

Moon Sign: Capricorn
Moon Phase: Second Quarter
Moon enters Aquarius 12:05 pm

☿ October 12

National Day (Spanish)
Waxing Moon
Color: Yellow

Moon Sign: Aquarius
Moon Phase: Second Quarter

♃ October 13

Yom Kippur
Waxing Moon
Color: Turquoise

Moon Sign: Aquarius
Moon Phase: Second Quarter
Moon enters Pisces 2:05 pm

♀ October 14

Battle Festival (Japan)
Waxing Moon
Color: Rose

Moon Sign: Pisces
Moon Phase: Second Quarter

♄ October 15

The October Horse (Roman)
Waxing Moon
Color: Indigo

Moon Sign: Pisces
Moon Phase: Second Quarter
Moon enters Aries 3:39 pm

☉ October 16

The Lion Sermon (British)
Waxing Moon
Color: Amber

Moon Sign: Aries
Moon Phase: Second Quarter

October 17 ☽

Pilgrimage to Paray-le-Monial
Waxing Moon
Color: Ivory

Moon Sign: Aries
Moon Phase: Full Moon 8:14 am
Moon enters Taurus 6:04 pm

October 18 ♂

Sukkot begins
Waning Moon
Color: Gray

Moon Sign: Taurus
Moon Phase: Third Quarter

October 19 ☿

Our Lord of Miracles Procession (Peruvian)
Waning Moon
Color: Brown

Moon Sign: Taurus
Moon Phase: Third Quarter
Moon enters Gemini 10:44 pm

October 20 ♃

Colchester Oyster Feast
Waning Moon
Color: Green

Moon Sign: Gemini
Moon Phase: Third Quarter

October 21 ♀

Feast of the Black Christ
Waning Moon
Color: White

Moon Sign: Gemini
Moon Phase: Third Quarter

October 22 ♄

Goddess of Mercy Day (Chinese)
Waning Moon
Color: Blue

Moon Sign: Gemini
Moon Phase: Third Quarter
Moon enters Cancer 6:41 am

October 23 ☉

Revolution Day (Hungarian)
Waning Moon
Color: Gold

Moon Sign: Cancer
Moon Phase: Third Quarter
Sun enters Scorpio 3:42 am

☽ October 24

United Nations Day · Sukkot ends
Waning Moon
Color: Silver

Moon Sign: Cancer
Moon Phase: Fourth Quarter 9:17 pm
Moon enters Leo 5:48 pm

♂ October 25

St. Crispin's Day
Waning Moon
Color: Scarlet

Moon Sign: Leo
Moon Phase: Fourth Quarter

☿ October 26

Quit Rent Ceremony (British)
Waning Moon
Color: White

Moon Sign: Aries
Moon Phase: Fourth Quarter

♃ October 27

Feast of the Holy Souls
Waning Moon
Color: Purple

Moon Sign: Aries
Moon Phase: Fourth Quarter
Moon enters Virgo 6:28 am

♀ October 28

Ochi Day (Greek)
Waning Moon
Color: Coral

Moon Sign: Virgo
Moon Phase: Fourth Quarter

♄ October 29

Iroquois Feast of the Dead
Waning Moon
Color: Black

Moon Sign: Virgo
Moon Phase: Fourth Quarter
Moon enters Libra 6:15 pm

☉ October 30

Daylight Saving Time ends
Waning Moon
Color: Orange

Moon Sign: Virgo
Moon Phase: Fourth Quarter

"Merlin" Faces British Court after Shopping with a Sword

Merlin Michael Williams appeared recently in a British court after being arrested for carrying a sword while shopping at a store in Portsmouth, England. A member of the Insular Order of the Druids, Williams was defended by another member of the order, King Arthur Pendragon. Other members appeared in court for support. All wore Druidic robes and regalia. Williams claimed precedent which had allowed Druids to carry ceremonial swords, and prosecutors eventually dropped the charges. The Crown Prosecution Service said that after due consideration, "it was deemed not to be in the public interest to continue with the case." No word as to whether Williams continues to wear his sword while shopping.

News Item

Psychic Visions of Profession's Future

Buck Wolf of ABC News asked several top psychics about the fate of their own profession, with varied and interesting responses. Well-known TV psychic Sylvia Browne says that extraterrestrials will be sending intergalactic messages with the help of clairvoyant translators by the year 2030. Lynn Robinson already hires out as an "intuitive consultant" to companies, and predicts this will be an emerging career field. Medium Jill Dahne senses that the next president will create a new Cabinet position, "Secretary of Foresight." And psychic Bayless Secord believes that in the near future, fortune tellers will be reading DNA just like reading palms.

October 31

Halloween · Samhain
Waning Moon
Color: Lavender

Moon Sign: Libra
Moon Phase: Fourth Quarter

November 2005

November 1

All Saints' Day
Waning Moon
Color: Gray

Moon Sign: Libra
Moon Phase: New Moon 8:25 pm
Moon enters Scorpio 2:29 am

November 2

All Souls' Day
Waxing Moon
Color: White

Moon Sign: Scorpio
Moon Phase: First Quarter

November 3

Ramadan ends
Waxing Moon
Color: Turquoise

Moon Sign: Scorpio
Moon Phase: First Quarter
Moon enters Sagittarius 8:55 am

November 4

Mischief Night (British)
Waxing Moon
Color: White

Moon Sign: Sagittarius
Moon Phase: First Quarter

November 5

Guy Fawkes Night (British)
Waxing Moon
Color: Blue

Moon Sign: Sagittarius
Moon Phase: First Quarter
Moon enters Capricorn 1:17 pm

November 6

Leonard's Ride (German)
Waxing Moon
Color: Amber

Moon Sign: Capricorn
Moon Phase: First Quarter

November 7 ☽

Mayan Day of the Dead
Waxing Moon
Color: Lavender

Moon Sign: Capricorn
Moon Phase: First Quarter
Moon enters Aquarius 4:31 pm

November 8 ♂

Election Day
Waxing Moon
Color: White

Moon Sign: Aquarius
Moon Phase: Second Quarter 8:57 pm

November 9 ☿

Lord Mayor's Day (British)
Waxing Moon
Color: Brown

Moon Sign: Aquarius
Moon Phase: Second Quarter
Moon enters Pisces 7:22 pm

November 10 ♃

Martin Luther's Birthday
Waxing Moon
Color: Purple

Moon Sign: Pisces
Moon Phase: Second Quarter

November 11 ♀

Veterans Day
Waxing Moon
Color: Coral

Moon Sign: Pisces
Moon Phase: Second Quarter
Moon enters Aries 10:22 pm

November 12 ♄

Tesuque Feast Day (Native American)
Waxing Moon
Color: Indigo

Moon Sign: Aries
Moon Phase: Second Quarter

November 13 ☉

Festival of Jupiter (Roman)
Waxing Moon
Color: Orange

Moon Sign: Aries
Moon Phase: Second Quarter

☽ November 14

The Little Carnival (Greek)
Waxing Moon
Color: Silver

Moon Sign: Aries
Moon Phase: Second Quarter
Moon enters Taurus 2:02 am

♂ November 15

St. Leopold's Day
Waxing Moon
Color: BlackTaurus

Moon Sign: Taurus
Moon Phase: Full Moon 7:58 pm

☿ November 16

St. Margaret of Scotland's Day
Waning Moon
Color: White

Moon Sign: Taurus
Moon Phase: Third Quarter
Moon enters Gemini 7:10 am

♃ November 17

Queen Elizabeth's Day
Waning Moon
Color: Crimson

Moon Sign: Gemini
Moon Phase: Third Quarter

♀ November 18

St. Plato's Day
Waning Moon
Color: Pink

Moon Sign: Gemini
Moon Phase: Third Quarter
Moon enters Cancer 2:42 pm

♄ November 19

Garifuna Day (Belizian)
Waning Moon
Color: Gray

Moon Sign: Cancer
Moon Phase: Third Quarter

☉ November 20

Commerce God Ceremony (Japanese)
Waning Moon
Color: Yellow

Moon Sign: Cancer
Moon Phase: Third Quarter

November 21 ☽

Repentance Day (German)
Waning Moon
Color: Ivory

Moon Sign: Cancer
Moon Phase: Third Quarter
Moon enters Leo 1:10 am

November 22 ♂

St. Cecilia's Day
Waning Moon
Color: Maroon

Moon Sign: Leo
Moon Phase: Third Quarter
Sun enters Sagittarius 12:15 am

November 23 ☿

St. Clement's Day
Waning Moon
Color: Topaz

Moon Sign: Leo
Moon Phase: Fourth Quarter 5:11 pm
Moon enters Virgo 1:41 pm

November 24 ♃

Thanksgiving Day
Waning Moon
Color: Green

Moon Sign: Virgo
Moon Phase: Fourth Quarter

November 25 ♀

St. Catherine of Alexandria's Day
Waning Moon
Color: Rose

Moon Sign: Virgo
Moon Phase: Fourth Quarter

November 26 ♄

Festival of Lights (Tibetan)
Waning Moon
Color: Black

Moon Sign: Virgo
Moon Phase: Fourth Quarter
Moon enters Libra 1:58 am

November 27 ☉

St. Maximus' Day
Waning Moon
Color: Gold

Moon Sign: Libra
Moon Phase: Fourth Quarter

☽   **November 28**
Day of the New Dance (Tibetan)   Moon Sign: Libra
Waning Moon   Moon Phase: Fourth Quarter
Color: Gray   Moon enters Scorpio 11:33 am

♂   **November 29**
Tubman's Birthday (Liberian)   Moon Sign: Scorpio
Waning Moon   Moon Phase: Fourth Quarter
Color: Red

☿   **November 30**
St. Andrew's Day   Moon Sign: Scorpio
Waning Moon   Moon Phase: Fourth Quarter
Color: Brown   Moon enters Sagittarius 5:32 pm

News Item

Courthouse Employees Are Ghostbusters

A new video security system installed at a Maryland courthouse on July 1, 2004, captured some images of a strange light roaming in a stairwell for over an hour on July 29. Though a security guard inspected the area and saw nothing, other guards in the monitor room watched as the light moved with the guard as he moved through the area. The investigating guard said he felt a chill once, which happened at the precise time the surveillance system showed the guard walking through the light. Other employees have described seeing odd shadows and hearing unexplained noises when nobody else was around. The security company says it was just a bug in the system, but many remain unconvinced.

December 2005

December 1

Big Tea Party (Japanese)
Waning Moon
Color: Purple

Moon Sign: Sagittarius
Moon Phase: New Moon 10:01 am

December 2

Republic Day (Laotian)
Waxing Moon
Color: Coral

Moon Sign: Sagittarius
Moon Phase: First Quarter
Sun enters Capricorn 8:42 pm

December 3

St. Francis Xavier's Day
Waxing Moon
Color: Brown

Moon Sign: Capricorn
Moon Phase: First Quarter

December 4   ☉

St. Barbara's Day
Waxing Moon
Color: Yellow

Moon Sign: Capricorn
Moon Phase: First Quarter
Moon enters Aquarius 10:26 pm

December 5

Eve of St. Nicholas' Day
Waxing Moon
Color: Silver

Moon Sign: Aquarius
Moon Phase: First Quarter

December 6

St. Nicholas' Day
Waxing Moon
Color: Black

Moon Sign: Aquarius
Moon Phase: First Quarter

December 7

Burning the Devil (Guatemalan)
Waxing Moon
Color: White

Moon Sign: Aquarius
Moon Phase: First Quarter
Moon enters Pisces 12: 44 am

December 8

Feast of the Immaculate Conception
Waxing Moon
Color: Turquoise

Moon Sign: Pisces
Moon Phase: Second Quarter 4:36 am

December 9

St. Leocadia's Day
Waxing Moon
Color: White

Moon Sign: Pisces
Moon Phase: Second Quarter
Moon enters Aries 4:02 am

December 10

Nobel Day
Waxing Moon
Color: Gray

Moon Sign: Aries
Moon Phase: Second Quarter

December 11

Pilgrimage at Tortugas
Waxing Moon
Color: Orange

Moon Sign: Aries
Moon Phase: Second Quarter
Moon enters Taurus 8:46 am

December 12

Fiesta of Our Lady of Guadalupe
Waxing Moon
Color: Lavender

Moon Sign: Taurus
Moon Phase: Second Quarter

December 13

St. Lucy's Day (Swedish)
Waxing Moon
Color: Maroon

Moon Sign: Taurus
Moon Phase: Second Quarter
Moon enters Gemini 2:59 pm

December 14

Warrior's Memorial (Japanese)
Waxing Moon
Color: Brown

Moon Sign: Gemini
Moon Phase: Second Quarter

December 15

Consualia (Roman)
Waxing Moon
Color: Green

Moon Sign: Gemini
Moon Phase: Full Moon 11:16 am
Moon enters Cancer 11:01 pm

December 16

Posadas (Mexican)
Waning Moon
Color: Pink

Moon Sign: Cancer
Moon Phase: Third Quarter

December 17

Saturnalia (Roman)
Waning Moon
Color: Blue

Moon Sign: Cancer
Moon Phase: Third Quarter

December 18
☉

Feast of the Virgin of Solitude
Waning Moon
Color: Amber

Moon Sign: Cancer
Moon Phase: Third Quarter
Moon enters Leo 9:18 am

☽ **December 19**

Opalia (Roman)
Waning Moon
Color: Gray

Moon Sign: Leo
Moon Phase: Third Quarter

♂ **December 20**

Commerce God Festival
Waning Moon
Color: Red

Moon Sign: Leo
Moon Phase: Third Quarter
Moon enters Virgo 9:39 pm

☿ **December 21**

Yule · Winter Solstice
Waning Moon
Color: Yellow

Moon Sign: Virgo
Moon Phase: Third Quarter
Sun enters Capricorn 1:35 pm

♃ **December 22**

Saints Chaeremon and Ischyrion's Day
Waning Moon
Color: Crimson

Moon Sign: Capricorn
Moon Phase: Third Quarter

♀ **December 23**

Larentalia (Roman)
Waning Moon
Color: Coral

Moon Sign: Capricorn
Moon Phase: Fourth Quarter 2:36 pm
Moon enter Libra 10:26 am

♄ **December 24**

Christmas Eve
Waning Moon
Color: Indigo

Moon Sign: Libra
Moon Phase: Fourth Quarter

☉ **December 25**

Christmas
Waning Moon
Color: Gold

Moon Sign: Libra
Moon Phase: Fourth Quarter
Moon enters Scorpio 9:04 pm

December 26

Kwanzaa begins · Hannukah begins
Waning Moon
Color: Ivory

Moon Sign: Scorpio
Moon Phase: Fourth Quarter

December 27

Boar's Head Supper (English)
Waning Moon
Color: Scarlet

Moon Sign: Scorpio
Moon Phase: Fourth Quarter

December 28

Holy Innocents' Day
Waning Moon
Color: Topaz

Moon Sign: Scorpio
Moon Phase: Fourth Quarter
Moon enter Sagittarius 3:43 am

December 29

St. Thomas à Becket's Day
Waning Moon
Color: White

Moon Sign: Sagittarius
Moon Phase: Fourth Quarter

December 30

Republic Day (Madagascar)
Waning Moon
Color: Purple

Moon Sign: Sagittarius
Moon Phase: New Moon 10:12 pm
Moon enters Capricorn 6:35 am

December 31 ♄

New Year's Eve
Waxing Moon
Color: Black

Moon Sign: Capricorn
Moon Phase: First Quarter

News Item

"Colorstrology" Reveals Daily Colors

Pantone, Inc. and author Michele Bernhardt have unveiled a new system that combines astrology, numerology, and color spirituality to form color profiles for every day of the year. Colorstrology takes traditional color research and moves it beyond science into the realm of metaphysics. Each day of the year has a unique color profile, as determined by the core traits of months and days including Sun Signs, daily numerological vibrations, and so on. Pantone, a recognized authority on color, has created a website (www.colorstrology.com) that offers free e-greetings based on the 366 daily personal colors and 21 monthly colors. They also are offering printed Colorstrology guides for each month.

January 2006

⊙   **January 1**

New Year's Day · Kwanzaa ends   Moon Sign: Capricorn
Waxing Moon   Moon Phase: First Quarter
Color: Yellow   Moon enters Aquarius 7:14 am

January 2 ☽

First Writing (Japanese)
Waxing Moon
Color: Gray

Moon Sign: Aquarius
Moon Phase: First Quarter

January 3 ♂

St. Genevieve's Day
Waxing Moon
Color: Red

Moon Sign: Aquarius
Moon Phase: First Quarter
Moon enters Pisces 7:43 am

January 4 ☿

Frost Fairs on the Thames
Waxing Moon
Color: Brown

Moon Sign: Pisces
Moon Phase: First Quarter

January 5 ♃

Epiphany Eve
Waxing Moon
Color: Green

Moon Sign: Pisces
Moon Phase: First Quarter
Moon enters Aries 9:44 am

January 6 ♀

Epiphany
Waxing Moon
Color: White

Moon Sign: Aries
Moon Phase: Second Quarter 1:56 pm

January 7 ♄

Rizdvo (Ukrainian)
Waxing Moon
Color: Indigo

Moon Sign: Aries
Moon Phase: Second Quarter
Moon enters Taurus 2:09 pm

January 8 ☉

Midwives' Day
Waxing Moon
Color: Orange

Moon Sign: Taurus
Moon Phase: Second Quarter

☽

January 9

Feast of the Black Nazarene (Filipino)
Waxing Moon
Color: Lavender

Moon Sign: Taurus
Moon Phase: Second Quarter
Moon enters Gemini 8:58 pm

♂

January 10

Business God's Day (Japanese)
Waxing Moon
Color: Black

Moon Sign: Gemini
Moon Phase: Second Quarter

☿

January 11

Carmentalia (Roman)
Waxing Moon
Color: White

Moon Sign: Gemini
Moon Phase: Second Quarter

♃

January 12

Revolution Day (Tanzanian)
Waxing Moon
Color: Turquoise

Moon Sign: Gemini
Moon Phase: Second Quarter
Moon enters Cancer 5:50 am

♀

January 13

Twentieth Day (Norwegian)
Waxing Moon
Color: Pink

Moon Sign: Cancer
Moon Phase: Second Quarter

♄

January 14

Feast of the Ass (French)
Waxing Moon
Color: Gray

Moon Sign: Cancer
Moon Phase: Full Moon 4:48 am
Moon enters Leo 4:31 pm

☉

January 15

Martin Luther King Jr.'s Birthday (actual)
Waning Moon
Color: Gold

Moon Sign: Leo
Moon Phase: Third Quarter

January 16

Martin Luther King Jr.'s Birthday (observed)
Waning Moon
Color: White

Moon Sign: Leo
Moon Phase: Third Quarter

January 17

St. Anthony's Day (Mexican)
Waning Moon
Color: Maroon

Moon Sign: Leo
Moon Phase: Third Quarter
Moon enters Virgo 4:49 am

January 18

Assumption Day
Waning Moon
Color: Yellow

Moon Sign: Virgo
Moon Phase: Third Quarter

January 19

Kitchen God Feast (Chinese)
Waning Moon
Color: Purple

Moon Sign: Virgo
Moon Phase: Third Quarter
Moon enters Libra 4:49 pm

January 20

Breadbasket Festival (Portuguese)
Waning Moon
Color: Rose

Moon Sign: Libra
Moon Phase: Third Quarter
Sun enters Aquarius 12:15 am

January 21

St. Agnes Day
Waning Moon
Color: Black

Moon Sign: Libra
Moon Phase: Third Quarter

January 22

Saint Vincent's Day
Waning Moon
Color: Amber

Moon Sign: Libra
Moon Phase: Fourth Quarter 10:14 am
Moon enters Scorpio 5:28 am

☽

January 23

St. Ildefonso's Day
Waning Moon
Color: Silver

Moon Sign: Scorpio
Moon Phase: Fourth Quarter

♂

January 24

Alasitas Fair (Bolivian)
Waning Moon
Color: Scarlet

Moon Sign: Scorpio
Moon Phase: Fourth Quarter
Moon enters Sagittarius 1:38 pm

☿

January 25

Burns' Night (Scottish)
Waning Moon
Color: Topaz

Moon Sign: Sagittarius
Moon Phase: Fourth Quarter

♃

January 26

Republic Day (Indian)
Waning Moon
Color: White

Moon Sign: Sagittarius
Moon Phase: Fourth Quarter
Moon enters Capricorn 5:31 pm

♀

January 27

Vogelgruff (Swiss)
Waning Moon
Color: Coral

Moon Sign: Capricorn
Moon Phase: Fourth Quarter

♄

January 28

St. Charlemagne's Day
Waning Moon
Color: Blue

Moon Sign: Capricorn
Moon Phase: Fourth Quarter
Moon enters Aquarius 6:09 pm

☉

January 29

Chinese New Year (dog)
Waning Moon
Color: Orange

Moon Sign: Aquarius
Moon Phase: New Moon 9:15 am

January 30 ☽

Three Hierarchs' Day (Eastern Orthodox)
Waxing Moon
Color: Ivory

Moon Sign: Aquarius
Moon Phase: First Quarter
Moon enters Pisces 5:32 pm

January 31 ♂

Islamic New Year
Waxing Moon
Color: Black

Moon Sign: Pisces
Moon Phase: First Quarter

——— February 2006 ———

February 1 ☿

St. Brigid's Day (Irish)
Waxing Moon
Color: Brown

Moon Sign: Pisces
Moon Phase: First Quarter
Moon enters Aries 5:46 am

February 2

Imbolc · Groundhog Day
Waxing Moon
Color: Green

Moon Sign: Aries
Moon Phase: First Quarter

February 3 ♀

St. Blaise's Day
Waxing Moon
Color: Pink

Moon Sign: Aries
Moon Phase: First Quarter
Moon enters Taurus 8:31 pm

February 4

Independence Day (Sri Lankan)
Waxing Moon
Color: Gray

Moon Sign: Taurus
Moon Phase: First Quarter

February 5 ☉

Festival de la Alcaldesa (Italian)
Waxing Moon
Color: Orange

Moon Sign: Taurus
Moon Phase: Second Quarter 1:29 am

☽

February 6

Bob Marley's Birthday (Jamaica)
Waxing Moon
Color: Lavender

Moon Sign: Taurus
Moon Phase: Second Quarter
Moon enters Gemini 2:32 am

♂

February 7

Full Moon Poya (Sri Lankan)
Waxing Moon
Color: Maroon

Moon Sign: Gemini
Moon Phase: Second Quarter

☿

February 8

Mass for Broken Needles (Japanese)
Waxing Moon
Color: Yellow

Moon Sign: Gemini
Moon Phase: Second Quarter
Moon enters Cancer 11:33 am

♃

February 9

St. Marion's Day (Lebanese)
Waxing Moon
Color: White

Moon Sign: Cancer
Moon Phase: Second Quarter

♀

February 10

Gasparilla Day (Florida)
Waxing Moon
Color: Rose

Moon Sign: Cancer
Moon Phase: Second Quarter
Moon enters Leo 10:44 pm

♄

February 11

Foundation Day (Japanese)
Waxing Moon
Color: Brown

Moon Sign: Leo
Moon Phase: Second Quarter

☉

February 12

Lincoln's Birthday (actual)
Waxing Moon
Color: Gold

Moon Sign: Leo
Moon Phase: Full Moon 11:44 pm

February 13

Parentalia (Roman)
Waning Moon
Color: Silver

Moon Sign: Leo
Moon Phase: Third Quarter
Moon enters Virgo 11:13 am

February 14

Valentine's Day
Waning Moon
Color: Gray

Moon Sign: Virgo
Moon Phase: Third Quarter

February 15

Lupercalia (Roman)
Waning Moon
Color: White

Moon Sign: Virgo
Moon Phase: Third Quarter

February 16

Fumi-e (Japanese)
Waning Moon
Color: Turquoise

Moon Sign: Virgo
Moon Phase: Third Quarter
Moon enters Libra 12:09 am

February 17

Quirinalia (Roman)
Waning Moon
Color: Coral

Moon Sign: Libra
Moon Phase: Third Quarter

February 18

Saint Bernadette's Second Vision
Waning Moon
Color: Blue

Moon Sign: Libra
Moon Phase: Third Quarter
Moon enters Scorpio 12:11 pm
Sun enters Pisces 2:24 pm

February 19
☉

Pero Palo's Trial (Spanish)
Waning Moon
Color: Yellow

Moon Sign: Scorpio
Moon Phase: Third Quarter

February 20

Presidents' Day
Waning Moon
Color: Ivory

Moon Sign: Scorpio
Moon Phase: Third Quarter
Moon enters Sagittarius 9:38 pm

February 21

Feast of Lanterns (Chinese)
Waning Moon
Color: Scarlet

Moon Sign: Sagittarius
Moon Phase: Fourth Quarter 2:17 am

February 22

Caristia (Roman)
Waning Moon
Color: Topaz

Moon Sign: Sagittarius
Moon Phase: Fourth Quarter

February 23

Terminalia (Roman)
Waning Moon
Color: Purple

Moon Sign: Sagittarius
Moon Phase: Fourth Quarter
Moon enters Capricorn 3:16 am

February 24

Regifugium (Roman)
Waning Moon
Color: White

Moon Sign: Capricorn
Moon Phase: Fourth Quarter

February 25

St. Walburga's Day
Waning Moon
Color: Black

Moon Sign: Capricorn
Moon Phase: Fourth Quarter
Moon enters Aquarius 5:14 am

February 26

Zamboanga Festival (Filipino)
Waning Moon
Color: Amber

Moon Sign: Aquarius
Moon Phase: Fourth Quarter

February 27 ☽

Threepenny Day
Waning Moon
Color: Gray

Moon Sign: Aquarius
Moon Phase: New Moon 7:31 pm
Moon enters Pisces 4:56 am

February 28 ♂

Mardi Gras (Fat Tuesday)
Waxing Moon
Color: Red

Moon Sign: Pisces
Moon Phase: First Quarter

March 2006

March 1 ☿

Ash Wednesday
Waxing Moon
Color: Yellow

Moon Sign: Pisces
Moon Phase: First Quarter
Moon enters Aries 4:18 am

March 2 ♃

St. Chad's Day (English)
Waxing Moon
Color: Green

Moon Sign: Aries
Moon Phase: First Quarter

March 3 ♀

Doll Festival (Japanese)
Waxing Moon
Color: Pink

Moon Sign: Aries
Moon Phase: First Quarter
Moon enters Taurus 5:22 am

March 4 ♄

St. Casimir's Day (Polish)
Waxing Moon
Color: Brown

Moon Sign: Taurus
Moon Phase: First Quarter

March 5 ☉

Isis Festival (Roman)
Waxing Moon
Color: Gold

Moon Sign: Taurus
Moon Phase: First Quarter
Moon enters Gemini 9:37 am

☽ March 6

Alamo Day
Waxing Moon
Color: Lavender

Moon Sign: Gemini
Moon Phase: Second Quarter 3:16 pm

♂ March 7

Bird and Arbor Day
Waxing Moon
Color: Black

Moon Sign: Gemini
Moon Phase: Second Quarter
Moon enters Cancer 5:38pm

☿ March 8

International Women's Day
Waxing Moon
Color: Brown

Moon Sign: Cancer
Moon Phase: Second Quarter

♃ March 9

Forty Saints' Day (Romanian)
Waxing Moon
Color: Purple

Moon Sign: Cancer
Moon Phase: Second Quarter

♀ March 10

Tibet Day
Waxing Moon
Color: Rose

Moon Sign: Cancer
Moon Phase: Second Quarter
Moon enters Leo 4:42 am

♄ March 11

Feast of Gauri (Hindu)
Waxing Moon
Color: Gray

Moon Sign: Leo
Moon Phase: Second Quarter

☉ March 12

Receiving the Water (Buddhist)
Waxing Moon
Color: Yellow

Moon Sign: Leo
Moon Phase: Second Quarter
Moon enters Virgo 5:23 pm

March 13 ☽

Purification Feast (Balinese)
Waxing Moon
Color: Gray

Moon Sign: Virgo
Moon Phase: Second Quarter

March 14 ♂

Mamuralia (Roman)
Waxing Moon
Color: Maroon

Moon Sign: Virgo
Moon Phase: Full Moon 6:35 pm

March 15 ☿

Phallus Festival (Japanese)
Waning Moon
Color: White

Moon Sign: Virgo
Moon Phase: Third Quarter
Moon enters Libra 6:12 am

March 16 ♃

St. Urho's Day (Finnish)
Waning Moon
Color: Turquoise

Moon Sign: Libra
Moon Phase: Third Quarter

March 17 ♀

St. Patrick's Day
Waning Moon
Color: Coral

Moon Sign: Libra
Moon Phase: Third Quarter
Moon enters Scorpio 5:59 pm

March 18 ♄

Sheelah's Day (Irish)
Waning Moon
Color: Blue

Moon Sign: Scorpio
Moon Phase: Third Quarter

March 19 ☉

St. Joseph's Day (Sicilian)
Waning Moon
Color: Amber

Moon Sign: Scorpio
Moon Phase: Third Quarter

The Wicca Wide Web

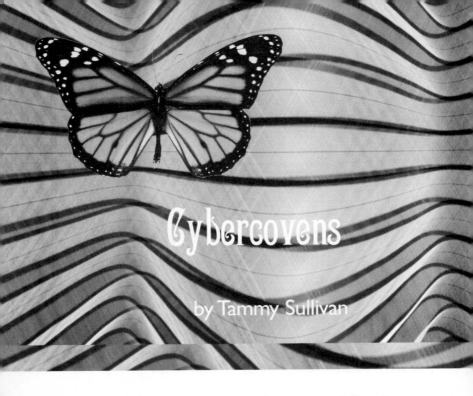

Cybercovens

by Tammy Sullivan

There is a distinct trend forming among the newer generation of Wiccans today. They are signing up in record numbers to join cybercovens. Cybercovens are hot, hip, and happening.

A cybercoven is a group of three or more like-minded Wiccans or Witches who come together over the Internet to celebrate Sabbats, work magic, or simply study and learn together. The size of such gatherings ranges from smaller groups of three members to larger cybercovens that number in the hundreds.

And these groups have quite diverse interests. For every conceivable twist on

the path, there will be a cybercoven or two to choose that travels that road. For instance some cybercovens, such as the Alexandrian cybercoven, are based on well-known traditions. Others are based on the elements, such as the Circle of the Sacred Flame cybercoven. And still others choose a more defining mark, such as taking primary lunar influence and calling the cybercoven the "Dark Witches" or some such name.

According to Lisa McSherry, who runs the website Cybercoven.org, evidence suggests that cybercovens have been operating since the mid-1980s when a set of enterprising Witches first began performing group rituals on CompuServe.

As the technology has improved by leaps and bounds since the '80s, the cybercovens of today have grown to be state of the art and fully functional. They have message boards set up for the members to discuss any and all related topics. They conduct rituals in chat and private messenger services. They usually have an e-mail list available as well.

Types of Cybercovens

There are several different types of cybercovens, each with different primary purposes. Included among them are teaching covens and groups that have the primary focus of educating the new generation. Many of the teaching covens function in the same manner as traditional earth-based covens. Often, they incorporate a large number of classes, texts, and exams.

Another type of cybercoven is the worship-based coven, sometimes referred to as a circle. Circles come together in celebration and faith, and they generally focus primarily on ritual.

There are also intimate covens formed by longtime friends who, for whatever reasons, are unable to get together for rituals in their real lives and must rely on the Internet.

Finally, there are covens that come together online strictly to work with and learn about magic. They may call themselves techno-Pagans, and often they have unique ways of using the Internet and personal computers for magical functions. They do this by interacting with others online and also by the use of computer programs designed to boost spell-power.

Cybercovens are hot, hip, and happening.

Some of the cybercovens operate with a traditional system and have a high priest or priestess in charge. Others may have a group of elders who attend to the day-to-day decision-making and keep the coven running smoothly by working together as a team. Usually, this is a democratic group, and decisions are subject to a vote.

Of all of the cybergroups currently in place today, the one that is the best established is the Coven of the Far Flung Net (CFFN). High priestess Kaatryn MacMorgan has been quoted as saying, "Faith is the first priority of our online group. CFFN focuses on ethics and a relationship with the divine."

The Coven of the Far Flung Net has been around since 1997, an eternity by today's Internet standards, where websites frequently don't last through their first month. The second-most established is the Jaguar Moon cybercoven, which has been operative since the year 2000. Jaguar Moon's High Priestess Lisa McSherry describes this group as a "teaching and information-sharing coven with rituals as components."

Cybercoven Participation

Many Wiccans who began their path as solitary practitioners out of necessity are now searching for groups to learn and grow with. Many people prefer the anonymity and safety that the Internet provides. Some seekers who are just beginning to walk their spiritual path are choosing to learn in a more traditional structure and begin their lessons by joining a teaching cybercoven. Often, they have no local source of information or few travel opportunities due to circumstances or health conditions. The Internet often is the only learning outlet available to them.

Cybercovens give the solitary Witch the best of both worlds. Not only can one experience the magic of group ritual, but one can do it from the comfort, privacy, and safety of the home.

Participating in online rituals can be deeply satisfying. Visualization and faith plays heavily into the field of online ritual. By faith I mean faith in both the divine and in your coven mates. A cybercoven ritual is usually written in advance and is available for all to study. Then, a a date and time is set for everyone to join in on the cyber-ritual. Members will meet in a specified chat room or create a private room exclusively for the ritual. In practice, the participants try to set up a working altar as closely as possible to the computer, and all of the coven members then perform the ritual together. Many groups focus their webcams on the altar so guests and participants can see exactly what they are doing and follow along.

Cybercoven elder Ocalee says this works to his great advantage. "As I am normally a solitary Witch, participating in group rituals online gives me a sense of belonging. I get to take part in something I can only read about otherwise."

Included in online ritual is the traditional Wiccan structure of casting a circle, calling the elements, partaking cakes and ale, making an invocation, and, depending on the ritual purpose, raising the cone of power. While the participants may verbalize their circle calls, invocations, and so on, they must also type it

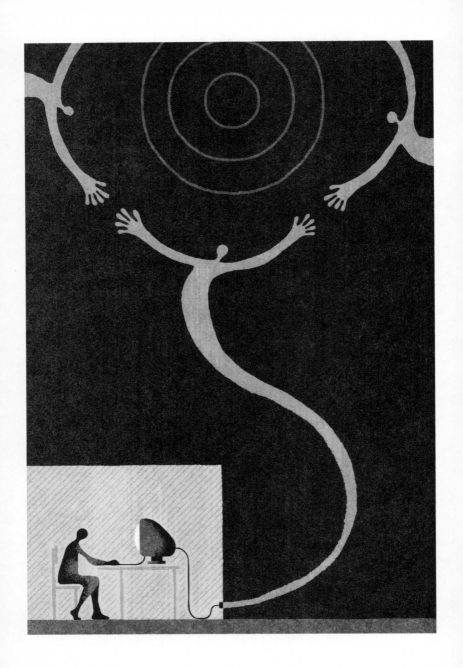

into the chat module so that the other members can follow along. You might think that all this cyberactivity and focus on the computer is a bit distracting, but in reality the nature of cybercover gatherings and rituals in fact seems to help keep members well focused.

In order to enhance the experience of rituals held online, many people choose to partake in spiritual cleansings beforehand and to wear their robes and circle jewelry during the actual ceremony. Often, people play music in their space during the ritual as well.

In addition to "chat" rituals, cybercovens organize "faith" rituals. A formal date and time is set for these, and ritual are sent to all coven members via e-mail or e-list. From there it is a matter of faith that all of the coven members are performing the working at the same time or soon afterward. These types of rituals are most often performed for Sabbats and as rituals of worship.

Navigating the Internet

The Internet has become an important resource for today's Wiccan. Information that was previously hard or impossible to find is now available for the seeker at the click of a mouse. As the new generation of Wicca grows, this information is now more important than ever. There is also a lot of misinformation found on the World Wide Web. For this reason, taking care when choosing a cybercoven choice is a must. It is imperative that you take the same amount of time with choosing a cybercoven as you would with choosing a traditional coven.

Accidentally joining the wrong group can be a horrendous event for the seeker, even if it's still a cybergroup. You can be abused, manipulated, and even outright deceived just as easily online as not. And such an event will call your faith into question. A sad byproduct of the cybercoven is the online abused Witches' shelter. These seem to be multiplying at a rapid rate, as the many Wiccans have no idea what to look for in joining a coven, and what to look out for.

It is very hard to accept that a spiritual group can be likened to a viper pit, but the wrong coven is just such a place. Take your time when checking out prospective covens, and be sure it is right for you before you commit yourself to it.

What to Look For

Here are some tips for joining a cybercoven.

1. The coven you are thinking of joining should match up as closely as possible with your beliefs. For example, if you work within a set pantheon, you will want a coven that works with the same, or similar, pantheon.

2. Check out the group dynamics. Are you allowed to express your opinion freely? Are you able to come and go as you please and as your schedule allows? Are there minimum time requirements of members? Can you meet those requirements?

3. Does the coven reflect your own basic morals and ethics?

4. Does the coven offer what you are seeking? Does it fit your primary needs? (In other words, make sure you aren't joining a working coven if you are in need of a teaching one.)

5. Is the primary purpose of the coven to come together to celebrate members' spirituality?

6. Does the coven accept everyone?

What to Look Out For

Here are some cybercoven warning signals.

1. Does the cybercoven allow you sufficient time to decide if it is the correct environment for you? Do they allow access into the inner workings of the coven while you are making your choice? If they do not, you may want to ask yourself what goes on behind closed doors and whether they are trying to hide petty fights and discord. (Keep in mind that certain things are supposed to remain private until you have advanced to a certain level.)

2. Do the high priestess or the elders use the coven as a personal political forum? A coven is not the place for espousing one's political views.

3. What happens in the case of disagreement with the ruling body of the coven? Will you be ostracized, criticized, or accused of being a "troublemaker"? Compare your prospective coven's response to that of Kat of CFFN: "We assume the student to be forthright, honest, and self-critical, but we want them to question our lessons, question our leaders, and ask 'why?' all the time. Perfect love and perfect trust is earned."

4. Be very careful of any coven leader who claims that the coven is based on a "vision." Unfortunately these visions can be delusions, and when you can't see the person proclaiming to have them face-to-face there is no way to know for sure. Sure, some visions are real, but not all are. When we are subject to a manipulative leader who is unethical and dishonest about such things, it directly affects our level of faith. Be very careful when dealing with this. The only vision you can truly rely on is your own.

5. Is the ruling body of the coven derogatory towards any members, former members, or other religions?

6. Is membership restricted to male or female only? Ask serious questions about this aspect of any coven. If one-sex-only is a trait you are seeking to include in your worship, you should still make sure it is not bigoted. In other words, you do not have to demean men in order to empower women, and vice versa. You must be careful that you do not find yourself in this sort of environment accidentally.

7. Be careful of groups that charge money. While modest dues are fair, there are groups out there that exist purely to make money off the seekers.

8. Be extremely aware of the elders, high priest, or high priestess. Pay attention to how they act and react. A power-tripping spiritual leader is an ugly thing, and one best avoided at all costs.

A Few Final Practical Tips

1. Always check out the background of the individuals in charge of the coven. Ask for personal references and places that they are

known within the online community. It is easy for anyone to design a web page and proclaim himself or herself a spiritual leader. A true leader will be pleased to know that you are taking your choice seriously enough to ask about their background, for it is a sign of a smart, sincere, and dedicated student. Only a phony or someone with something to hide would be offended.

2. Check the background of the cybercoven itself. Ask if you can speak with former members about why they left the group. If the coven is trying to hide embarrassing incidents they most likely will not allow you to have this information or they may turn down your membership just because you requested it. Console yourself with the knowledge that no true coven would behave this way, as they understand it is a two-way street when information is requested. At the same time, if you are allowed access to former members keep in mind that they may be biased. Take everything they say with a grain of salt and measure the words carefully.

3. Remember to play it safe. Coven or not, basic Internet safety rules still apply. Do not agree to meet other coven members alone and do not give them your personal information. The only people in need of your personal information are the elders or the high priestess—once you have learned to trust them.

4. Make a point to ask about curses. That is, has the group leader ever proclaimed themselves cursed by another? Have they tried to enlist the aid of the coven in canceling a curse or sending one? If so, run! This is a bad sign. No true coven leader will involve the members in dramatic games and plots against others, and they certainly will not fool around with curses. Beware of the leader who seeks to get you to perform magic in any form on their behalf.

5. A coven is not your family, support group, or twelve-step program. The coven environment may be supportive, but its primary purpose is spiritual growth. While you are concentrating on yours, the other members must concentrate on theirs. Do not drain their energy by constantly seeking support and complain-

ing about how miserable you are and how insurmountable are your problems. Eventually, they will tire of it and tell you to stop whining and do something about it (just as you would with someone saying such things to you).

6. If you are not willing to do the work, don't waste your time or the group's time. There is always a fair amount of work involved in any coven. Depending on your level of experience you may be required to take a class, write rituals, or even teach a class.

7. Keep in mind that at times it can be difficult to understand the tone of others in an online environment. What may seem insulting to you may not be intended that way. Honesty and bluntness go a long way online. If you aren't sure what someone means, ask!

8. Do not gossip. I have seen groups allow one individual to single-handedly ruin the sanctity of the circle for everyone by gossiping and complaining to others. When it comes to gossip, you will be found out and your removal from the group will be necessary. Gossip harms all involved. It ruins the mutual respect between members.

9. Finally, listen to your inner bell. If anything makes you nervous or jumpy in the coven environment take it as a signal from the divine that you are not meant to be there and go. Trust in divinity to lead you to your place.

Participating in a cybercoven and finding the right one for you is most often a richly rewarding experience, one unequaled in any other environment. I wish you the brightest of blessings on your personal cyber-journeys.

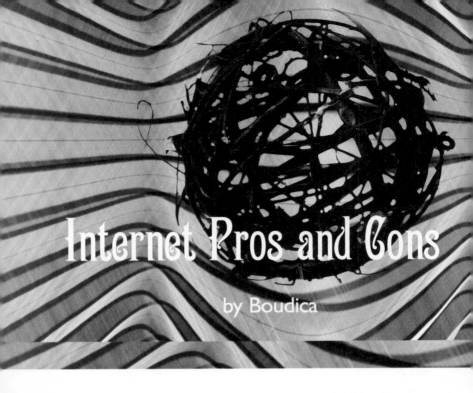

Internet Pros and Cons

by Boudica

The Pagan community hit the ground running when publishers started putting as many books as the public could buy on book store shelves in the 1970s. It became big business, and suddenly all manner of occult topics were hot sellers. The door to the age of information was opened, and there was no turning back.

The Internet was birthed by the military and some government institutions as a communication device. Through the late 1980s and into the early 1990s, it was pretty much an exclusive tool used only by a few with the access and technical savvy. It was at best a high-priced novelty.

Something unexpected was going on in the background during the early, experimental years of the Internet. Those who had been reading the occult books published by the popular Pagan press in the '70s and '80s were beginning to find each other via the Internet. First it was in chat rooms; then information was shared on websites.

Something unexpected was going on in the background—Pagans were finding each other via the Internet.

At one time during the late 1990s, the fastest growing types of websites were those considered "religious" in nature, and Pagan sites were among the most common such sites. The '90s saw the birth of numerous Pagan sites. They were visited not only by the Pagan population but also by people who were shocked that such things existed and by people who were just curious. The Internet became the new publishing tool for the Pagan population—now in a purely electronic format.

So again, the movement was given a whole new batch of information and was off and running.

The Internet as a Tool

As a tool, both books and the Internet have provided sources of useful information. Both have also been sources of some pretty silly junk.

Books helped to spread the "word" of the Pagan movement. Most memorable in my mind is first reading Margot Adler's *Drawing Down the Moon* and Starhawk's *Spiral Dance*. Everyone who was anyone read those two books back in the day, bought the revised editions when they came out, and spoke of them constantly in chat rooms and on websites.

The other books that made waves were Scott Cunningham's books on "Solitary Wicca." Not since Lady Sheba published in 1971 had there been so much brew-ha-ha about a published work. And we have not seen the like until now.

With the age of electronic media and its instant communication, suddenly whatever anyone can think of and dream up can be published on the Internet.

The use of the Internet as a communications tool is well documented even in its short life. Once it caught on and access became cheap enough for everyone to afford, there was no stopping the rush. By the late '90s Pagans were regularly finding other Pagans on the Internet. There are entire areas in many of the ISPs (Internet service providers) where Pagans can have private chat, run their own bulletin boards, list their websites, and communicate via e-groups.

We also quickly discovered a few things about the Internet. For one, we learned there were a lot more Pagans than we had thought. Sit in any Pagan chat room on a class night and you would see the screen names of sixty or seventy Pagans. Most nights, there are twenty or more regular chatters. And that's just on one chat room—there are many spread across the ether on such services as Prodigy, AOL, CompuServe, and Excite.com. There are even chat rooms setups as part of private websites.

But the question is: what goes on in these chat rooms and on these websites? Well, for one, Pagans are connecting with other Pagans both nationally and locally. This was the foundation from which many of our established web groups formed. Many local Pagans would also get together outside the chat rooms in what are now known as "Pagan Nights Out," where they would meet at bookstores or coffee shops and get to know each other personally. The Internet led to real life for many. The connections led to people getting to know other and to form groups—some in real life, some in cyberspace.

The movement built so quickly that holes in information were being filled in by those who were less credible. It was spread in chat rooms, and it was spread on websites.

The main attraction and the biggest problem with the Internet? Anonymity. Here, one can declare his or her Paganism, spirituality, and tradition, yet one cannot be readily identified. On

the Internet, we are secret and public at the same time. It's a strange middle ground that can lead to confusion and occasional abuse.

Pagan Uses for the Internet

Pagan information sites sprang up in the early days of the Internet like tulips in May. Everyone posted correspondences charts and the charge of the Goddess (though most didn't know who wrote their particular version). Many sites were run by someone claiming to be Lord this or Lady that, and you could pick out the newbie violating copyrights by posting entire books to their websites. Anything and everything was declared valid.

But was this what we wanted? We did want the freedom to express ourselves, and these websites gave us the ability. However, the web also perpetuated myths, misinformation, and it helped spread out-and-out lies. And no one was able to hold anyone accountable, because we were all masked with Internet nicknames and ghost ISPs.

There is a need for religion to grow and evolve. There is a need for religion to fill the needs of seekers. But the myth-information aspect of the Internet is suddenly a big problem. People have taken to abusing the freedom of the web, cloaking themselves in terminology such as "religious tolerance" and "freedom of expression."

Among the problems: We find Wicca on many websites reduced to a "goodness and light" theology, forced into a false monotheism in order to make the polytheistic ideal acceptable to the norm. The Internet has been a prime force in movements to adapt Pagan beliefs and make them palatable to a mainstream. As a result, we've ended up with the "hyphenated practitioners," who have little idea what they are doing, and who are unaware that they are disrespecting several deities in their attempt to keep themselves happy.

Paganism has evolved on the web from a lifestyle to a religion. Tattoos have become *the* tribal art for people who have no tribe; piercings are rights of passage for people who have no common community. And still, we do not speak a common language when it comes to much of our terminology. Everyone seems to be making it up as they go along. The web has produced a cyber-community for people who have no attachments to community in real life.

There is much to be said for diversity. While the web presents us with a plethora of different viewpoints, it also allows us to justify our right to be anything we choose

Still, there is dogma to many religions. Should we ignore the dogma because someone's website says you can ignore it? While being Pagan means you can choose for yourself whatever spiritual path you prefer, does that mean you can apply this notion to other religions, mixing and matching to suit your needs?

Once these notions have been written on the web, and so become perpetuated through repeated viewing in e-mails, bulletin boards, and other websites, does this make the ideas any more valid?

If you wish to walk your own spiritual path, go ahead. You can make your own choices, and you are welcome to believe them valid for yourself. But your choice to believe what you believe does not make changing an established dogma correct. Yes, the new idea becomes your own adaptation, your own standard. But it does not apply to another's idea or standards. Just because you have reinvented the hot dog, it does not entitle you to call it Oscar Mayer. It is just your hot dog, and it's really only good for you.

Spreading Fiction

I haven't said anything about the creation of religious tenets from fiction. It's certainly possible, and valid, that we may like the philosophy we see adapted in a movie or book. But the question is, can we actually live fiction? The basic question is, if it appeals to many, does that mean it is valid as a religion?

In the last British census, 390,000 people claimed "Jedi Knight" in declaring their religion. While there are some who did this in jest, what about the rest? We come to a dilemma. Do we need to support their claim by acknowledging their right to religious freedom, or is this a case where we might be justified in declaring the emperor has no clothes?

This brings up further issues regarding insular societies and what Cass Sunstein refers to as the "echo chamber" effect. Modern humans live such complicated lives generally that we choose to associate with those who we feel best represent and uphold ideas we already feel comfortable with. We insulate ourselves from those who try to discuss anything other than what we firmly believe—no matter how rational, realistic, or logical the discussion. And of course we see this misguided attitude in many e-groups and chat rooms.

As a result, we "echo" the voice of our group, no matter whether right or wrong. How many times have we heard someone yell that their religious rights were violated, and ten minutes later the news is spread all over the web in every e-mail group, website, and chat room. Of course, more often than not, once someone takes the time to investigate the issue it is discovered that the cry of violation is a ruse to cover up that the person was breaking the law or doing something unethical. When this happens, the entire community ends up with egg on their faces. The community may even spend money to retain lawyers for this wolf-crying, thus in the end wasting precious time and resources.

In many instances on the Internet, we also echo popular sentiment. An article by law professor Cass Sunstein reveals that when multiple conflicting ideas or opinions occur in a group, the minority will shift to the majority opinion. If I believe that the God and Goddess are separate individuals in my view of deity, but the majority of the list believes that God and Goddess are two facets of the same singular deity, I will be more likely to express the singular belief than the duality belief when with my own group. So much then for freedom of religion and expression when stuck in a vibrating echo chamber.

But this is not the way of all groups, Internet or otherwise. There are always individuals who will not shift their view to the majority's, and who have firm beliefs. There are groups that can express and discuss individual ideas and beliefs, voice opinions regardless of what the majority believes, and allow room for personal expression. And to be even more interesting, these individuals and groups are not as scarce as you may think.

Tolerant Internet Groups

Groups that encourage discussion of ideas that are truly diverse are all around the country. These people are educated in the history and essence of our spirituality and the methods of the established spiritual paths. They know what they speak of and find that diversity can be shared, discussed, and established without polluting the origins of the belief systems that were put in place. They also have learned how to evolve our spirituality into a belief system that meets our needs without having to lose the original ideas and ideals that started the movement in the first place. They hold their own ideas and opinions without becoming beholden to the echo effect.

There is a difference between being intolerant and refusing to validate what we see as being a personal spirituality system. Anyone can tolerate another's choice of spiritual path, but we can only validate that which we have personal knowledge of and have experienced. I cannot validate your particular spiritual path if I have not experienced your spirituality.

This is because we all have our own path to deity. If someone comes to me with a spirituality that I have experienced, this I can validate. To expect otherwise is like asking me to review a book based on the title. I cannot review the book if I have not read it. I need to experience the book first before I can comment.

In order for this community to expand and continue to grow, we need to realize the Internet has given us much to work with and much we need to sort out. We need to understand the basics of what has gone before us in order to keep the flavor of the old ways while we look to keep the religion evolving and changing just enough to meet people's needs.

We need to understand the difference between religious choice and religious tolerance. We need to understand that we can expect tolerance of our choices but we will not necessarily receive validation.

We need to avoid being insular. We have the right to our own path of spirituality, but we should not force others to our choice, nor should they expect us to follow their beliefs just because we associate with them. The idea of religious freedom is that all paths are the right path, and we are free to walk them as we choose. That you and I should walk the same path for a while does not mean we are the same, just that we are sharing the road.

And finally, with all the information that is available to us on the Internet, always ask yourself, what value does this information have to yourself or your community? All information needs to be reviewed, and you need to take personal responsibility for deciding its true value.

Over the Cauldron

Up-to-date Wiccan
opinions & rantings
overheard & spelled
out just for you

Recycling Personal Energy

by Cerridwen Iris Shea

"Thoughts are things."

"Be careful what you wish for."

"The energy you put out comes back three times."

It's enough to make you want to turn off your brain sometimes. All of the above aphorisms are valid, important points in our practice. However, what happens when we have a bad day? We can't be wonderful, perfect beings of light all the time. If we were, we wouldn't be here. We'd be—well, wherever our individual belief systems

place us when we attain that level of enlightenment. We're here, we're human, and we're not perfect. We try to work within our ethical codes, and sometimes it just doesn't work.

Fear and guilt from not being the "perfect Pagan" can hurt us. It can eat away at our self-esteem and can make us worry that we're not "real" Pagans or Witches. Ultimately, it can make us sick. At the same time, pretending to be perfect also has consequences. Repressing negative feelings causes them to fester within, bringing pain, decay, and even more serious illness.

Bad days are just going to happen. There's going to be a time when someone cuts you off in a car or is rude to you just when you can't stand one more irritation. How often is the phrase "eat &*!$ and die!" used in our culture on a daily basis? Do we want the person literally to eat something unpleasant and die? Rarely. We want retribution for the person's behavior. Sometimes the anger we feel is out of proportion to the actual situation. But we still have those feelings. We still throw the thought out there before we restrain ourselves. So what do we do when we have a bad day?

If thoughts are things, that means we've wished someone harm. We've created the thought and therefore created the reality that we want the person who ran over our toe with the shopping cart to die. How often do we wish others to cease living in this world? Not only is it not our right to make that choice over someone else's future, but doing so stains our own karma. If we get back three times what we put out, what is our retribution? Will we die? Will our biggest fears manifest?

Should we stop to sort out every thought, every action, every word? Of course we should. But the reality of life is that sometimes we will react, and sometimes those reactions will be negative. Most of the time, we don't literally want the person to die. We want the person to leave us alone.

Anger is not the only disturbing emotion we feel. We feel grief, envy, anxiety. Trapping ourselves in those emotions will pull us into the maelstrom of despair. Repressing and refusing to acknowledge them will do the same.

So how do we express emotions that can hurt us in a healthy way without causing harm, especially if we believe "thoughts are things"?

We recycle our personal energy. We take those emotions, acknowledge them, and transform them into something that enhances our lives rather than decimates them.

Meditation and self-exploration play a part in the exercise. It's helpful to have your magical journal (separate from your Book of Shadows) and a piece of paper that you can burn. This can be done as a full ritual, or simply by encircling yourself in protective, positive energy. It is important that you create safe space in which to experience your grief, rage, and fear. You want to be able to let go of the energy without leaving yourself open to negative influences. By keeping the energy within sacred space to recycle it, you not only protect yourself but you keep from inflicting "drive-by" energy on anyone else. We've all been hit with that kind of energy. Have you ever walked past people and suddenly felt inexplicably angry, depressed, or sad? That's "drive-by" energy. Many people don't realize that's what they actively send out. As magical practitioners, part of our responsibility is to be aware when we experience those emotions and avoid inflicting them on anyone else.

I go to Kuan Yin for help. Since she is a goddess of mercy, compassion, and forgiveness, her stabilizing and gentle presence keeps the space anchored.

Bad days are just going to happen.

Use a fireproof dish and have a piece of paper on which you can list your emotions and burn them.

Once you're safely within sacred space, take a few minutes to ground, center, and breathe. Count three sets of ten, with inhalations as odd numbers and exhalations as even numbers. Concentrate on the number and let everything else float away. The counting will keep the noise and clutter from taking over your mind.

When you're finished your three sets of ten, let your mind wander a bit. Try not to follow any linear thought process. Simply see where your thoughts take you.

Do another three sets of ten breaths.

Tell Kuan Yin what's bothering you. State the situation simply, without trying to defend or justify it. Give the facts: This happened, then that happened, then I wanted to say or do this. Admit it if you sent out negative energy, and ask that the energy be gathered back up for recycling, with harm to none.

Now that you've said it, explore it. Why did the situation upset you? What feelings and thoughts did it trigger? Did it really have anything to do with the other person, or did it remind you of something else upsetting that happened in your past? What fears, insecurities, or angers does the situation touch on?

Did you take every calm, physical action that you could to change the situation? For instance, if you felt threatened, did you report it to the proper authorities? Did you remove yourself from the situation? Did you take proper precautions? If it the situation was less threatening, but still potentially dangerous—

such as someone cutting in front of you on the highway—did your brakes work properly? Do you need to take your car in for maintenance? If it was a hurtful comment at a cocktail party, does the speaker actually matter in your life? Is this someone you don't have to deal with in the future?

Explore, explore, explore. Take the situation apart. Look at all the pieces. Figure out how much importance it has in your life. Often, when we do that, we find that the situation that triggered the feelings isn't that important. However, there's something behind it that is. Find out what it is, and see what you can do to resolve it.

Sometimes, it's a case of being aware that there's a bigger issue behind the initial reaction, and it's an issue that will take time to resolve. That's okay. Not everything can be fixed in a single ritual. But at least you're aware of the foundation and can figure out how to take care of the root. If an old tree is rotten and about to fall on your house, stripping off one leaf won't solve the problem. You have to remove the entire tree.

Now you have a bit more balance and perspective on the situation. Write out all the feelings on the piece of paper. Set it on fire and let it burn. Watch the smoke rise and imagine the feelings dissipating into the air.

Once the fire is safely out, close your eyes and take a few deep breaths. Imagine the negative energy leaving your body, seeping into the earth where it will be recycled by Gaia into something good. You don't have to specify what that is—you are simply returning energy to the earth for transformation. Gaia will decide how to use it. When you're hit with drive-by negativity, you can also imagine the energy passing through you into the ground, for Gaia's recycling. Don't buy into it. Don't hold onto it. Let it pass through you without tainting your essence.

Now, open your eyes. You should feel as though you've had a full cleansing. Ground and center, give thanks, make an offering, and close the circle. If you've dealt with a small annoyance, you can let go of it and continue your day. If you've discovered

that this was the indication of a larger, longer-term problem, start taking the steps to resolve it. Either way, you have acknowledged your feelings and taken responsibility for them.

When you're caught in a situation and fling out negativity, take a minute to breathe. There's nothing wrong in saying to spirit, "I'm having a hard time today. I don't feel like a loving, light, tolerant person. I'm angry. I have a right to be angry."

It's not about justifying the negativity. Part of the growth process is to learn how to deal with negativity, not return negative with negative. This doesn't mean becoming a doormat. What it means is gaining perspective on each individual situation and making the most ethical response you can. When you know you have an ethical conflict, take it to spirit. Don't try to defend yourself. Just say, "This is the situation. I'm having trouble with it. Help me."

And then listen. Don't search for the response you want in order to excuse your behavior or thought process. Listen to the real answer. Look around you. What is the next animal that crosses your path? What is the fragment of song or conversation that you hear? It could apply to your situation. And it might seem completely ridiculous at the time, but make sense later.

We try to live our paths mindfully. That means a combination of thinking and feeling, based in a firm ethical foundation. This allows us to live in the moment, whether those feelings are positive or negative. It also allows us to make informed, responsible decisions. Recycling your energy is yet another way to make the planet—and the part of the planet that is yourself—whole.

Walking Our Talk

by Dianne Sylvan

You probably think this is yet another article about the Wiccan Rede. And maybe, yes, I'll throw in a bit about the Threefold Law and warn you that everything you do comes back to you three times over. But I won't force it down your throat. For, as you know, books on Wicca go on and on and on about ethics, telling you not to hex people or do anything manipulative—before getting back to the far more interesting business of casting spells and dancing naked on Sabbats.

I am not going to bore you. Any "Wicca 101" book you've read will have told you all you need to know about ethics, and if you're like me you're probably sick to death of reading the same messages over and over again. Also, I will say ethics is just not as simple as it seems.

Once you make the decision to live as a Wiccan and dedicate yourself as a priest or priestess of the Lord and Lady, you will realize that that whole "harm none" thing is hard to apply to modern life, and the Threefold Law, well, just doesn't tend to work out the way we'd like. If someone hurts you he won't necessarily get three times that hurt back. Sometimes the bad guys win, and sometimes you make decisions that end up backfiring in surprising and unpleasant ways. No matter if you're Wiccan, Christian, Jew, atheist—life occasionally sucks for one and all.

Still, Wicca has very little in the way of dogma. The Rede is probably our closest thing to scripture, our own extremely condensed Ten Commandments. Even then, as you may already know, the word *rede* itself means "counsel or guidance." This, of course, offers us incredible freedom to make our own decisions, but it also means we have to make our own decisions.

Most of us come from religious and social backgrounds with a lot of rules and thou-shalt-nots, and we are used to having most of our ethical choices predetermined. I've found that even the supposedly hard and fast rules have a tendency to wobble a little when, say, you're confronted with someone who plans to harm your loved ones. "Thou shalt not kill" ends up taking a back seat to "Thou shalt not mess with my family." This is, of course, because although some systems like to pretend the world is black and white, in reality it is mostly shades of gray.

The Rede is an excellent guiding force for our lives, and a backbone to our ethical system, but it is incomplete. With the concept of karmic return, we have a good overall ideal (in general, "Don't be a jerk"), but not much to help us in our day-to-day lives. Most of the time our ethical dilemmas aren't simple enough to simply "do what you will, as it harms none." After all, how do you define harm? And how can you know what another person considers harmful? Where does the line fall between self-defense and retribution? For instance, if you get a job that means someone else who applied didn't get it. Is that harm?

If we use nothing but the Rede as our ethical system, we run the real risk of becoming paralyzed by a fear of causing harm, and our lives are less lived than avoided. We can't sit and smile at the squirrels **I am not going to bore you. Any "Wicca 101" book will have told you all you need to know about ethics.** all day. We have to get out into the world and be a positive force for change and to manifest our deities as best we can. Eventually we all have to figure out how to limit our own behavior and act properly in various circumstances. Those boundaries will vary for each of us.

I personally interpret the Rede as a balance. That is, one should balance the "harm" you do just by walking on the ground and breathing the air with a positive and healing effect. To quote the Prayer of St. Francis, "Where there is hatred, let me sow love." To that end, I sat down one night to try to hash out my own personal ethical code, based on what I understand Wicca to be—a living, vibrant spirituality that encourages its practitioners to grow, evolve, and be an agent of deity in daily life.

Wiccan philosophy views the manifest universe as an expression of the divine. When you look at the world from that point of view, you won't need someone to tell you it's wrong to kill or steal. It pretty much goes without saying that violating another's free will is also a violation of the person's divine nature. Newcomers to Wicca may want more concrete advice, but in the end we have to decide how to live the Rede and how to create our own ethical system.

What I came up with was an idea I call the Wiccan Graces. These are your own personal set of ethical and spiritual tenets, abstract concepts you strive to bring into the real world through your actions and words. The Graces form the outer structure of your standards of behavior, with the Rede and karmic return as their inner framework. They give you goals to work toward and core values to manifest through your ritual and magic.

So think about the kind of Wiccan you want to be. What are your values? How will you act as the hands of the Lord and Lady on Earth? This is a hard question, and one that no one can answer for you. The focus of your spiritual life might be very different from someone else's. For example, you may feel called to teach public Wicca classes or start a coven, while a friend might prefer volunteering in the community when she can.

You might not even be in a place where you are even ready to think about contributing to the larger world directly; that's fine. The first few years of your practice will most likely be devoted to your own spiritual growth, and this is imperative. If you place your focus on the community without first having a strong practice, your efforts will be hollow and eventually collapse under people's expectations. Not everyone is a teacher or a leader, and forcing yourself to be one won't help anyone. By becoming a self-actualized practitioner of Wicca, you will influence the community.

Once you have thought about your Graces, write them out in your Book of Shadows, preferably on the first page or somewhere prominent so you'll often be reminded what you are working toward. Write a list of single words or phrases, along the lines of a pledge or creed. I recommend creating a ritual rededication in which you declare your intent to the universe to follow these Graces to the best of your ability.

Here, then, are my own Graces, to get you started, as well as a bit of discussion on why each is important to my path. Don't follow them slavishly—as I said, yours might be quite different. Use these as a starting point to create your own. Don't be afraid to change them as you change. Your standards should grow with you, and ideally you should be setting higher goals as you learn and grow.

Wiccan Graces

Love. On my path, the very essence of deity is love. While I might not be capable of the kind of unconditional and all-accepting love that the God and Goddess have shown me, I can still try my hardest to love as they do. Love is the underlying energy of the cosmos that informs and strengthens all the Graces to follow. If I can look at the world and my fellow travelers from a place of love, nothing life throws at me can knock me over for long.

Compassion. Compassion is the immediate outgrowth of love. It's also very, very hard on the heart. The minute we take off society's earn-and-spend blinders, we can see all the suffering and sorrow around us. This realization can lead us to step out of the mainstream of consumerist culture to dedicate our lives to making conditions better. Still, one person can only help so much. If I can only help one person in my whole life, that's one more person than was helped before. Compassion can be overwhelming and painful, but without it, our service to the gods becomes rote and empty.

Forgiveness. This is another Grace that Westerners (and some other cultures) don't particularly appreciate. But there's nothing holy about a grudge. As hard as it is to forgive someone (including yourself), in the end it's much harder to carry around the burden of anger and bitterness. These eventually become poison that darkens our eyes to the beauty of the world.

Humor. I'm definitely not a Wiccan who enjoys dour and somber ritual. It's hard not to laugh when you completely forget all your carefully written words mid-invocation and have to settle for, "Hello there, Goddess! If you're not busy, could you come play with us a while? Um . . . Merry meet!" I take my religion seriously, but never myself. The universe is way too absurd not to laugh at it. Just look at the giraffe.

Gratitude. Our parents' first lessons in manners usually teach us to say "please" and "thank you." Why do most of us forget this the minute we leave home? The sun came up today, you didn't get hit by a train, and you can read. Be thankful! I try to make a practice of giving thanks for a new day when I wake up, no matter what I'm facing in the next twelve hours. Each time you

wake up you have a chance to do better than the day before. It's a miracle we even exist in the vast black expanse of space, much less have opposable thumbs—so a little gratitude is a good thing.

Integrity. You could replace this one with "honesty," but I've found that total honesty is nearly impossible in this day and age without crushing someone's feelings. Integrity is saying what you mean and meaning what you say, rather than saying whatever is "true." People who go in for "brutal honesty" are usually only brutal. There's something to be said for tact.

Wisdom. Where I grew up we had two kinds of "smartness"— book learning and common sense. Often people with a lot of one had none of the other. In this case, however, I'm speaking of the knowledge that comes with experience of both. Wisdom is taking the words of others and combining them with what you have seen and felt—thus considering equally both valuable teachers.

Joy. Joy isn't something we can sustain 24-7 without heavy drugs or light insanity, so it's vital that we learn to cherish the unexpected joys of life. One thing I like to do when I am feeling depressed is to start making a list of "things that make me happy." This runs the gamut from the color of my favorite nail polish to the way oak trees always sound sleepy when they speak to me. It's easy to get bogged down in sorrow and darkness in this world. Remembering joy can create more joy.

Growth. I have met Pagans who reached ten years of practice and simply stopped growing. They had figured out their practices, read all the books they felt they needed to, and settled in to doing the same old thing year after year. If nature is our greatest teacher, the Goddess manifest, then stagnating in our growth runs against her ways. I constantly strip off the clothes that no longer fit me and work to weave new ones. There is no other way to live.

There are, of course, other Graces you could add to this list: strength, power, balance, activism, and service, just to name a few. It's up to you to decide what is important to you. Never forget that you are an embodiment of divine energy and grace. Walk your talk as only the God or Goddess could.

A Pledge to the Lord and Lady

I who am a priest/ess, Witch, and child of the God and Goddess, do hereby resolve:

I will walk upon the world lightly, striving for balance in all things.
I will strive for integrity and act with mindfulness.
I will look for the blessings and humor in all my wanderings.
I will come from a place of love for all of creation.
I will look to nature and her wisdom for guidance.
I will be a source of strength and comfort to my family.
I will choose healing over harm, and remember that the choice is mine alone to make.

So mote it be.

Is This a New Aquarian Age?

by Emely Flak

We have all heard about the Age of Aquarius in articles and in the words to the famous song from the 1970s stage musical *Hair*. Although this well-known song is beautiful and uplifting, the lyrics fail to explain what this Aquarian Age really means. If we listen to the lyrics, we hear that "Jupiter aligns with Mars," but there is greater significance to the Aquarian Age that we should all be aware of.

The Age of Aquarius is similar to another phenomenon we've all long been exposed to—the "New Age." In fact, the term itself gets its name from the coming of new astrological Age of Aquarius. Although we've been hearing about Aquarius and the New Age for some years now, there are many questions I'm often asked about these terms. What does the new astrological age really mean? What is its significance in terms of social change and shifts in mindset? How does it relate to the growth of alternative spirituality? What is this New Age optimism all about? More importantly, is the New Age an age for Paganism and Wicca?

The Astrological Ages

Each astrological age spans around 2,000 to 2,500 years. Currently, it is believed that we are on the cusp of a brilliant new optimistic era identified as the Aquarian Age. The astrological ages occur in reverse order to the zodiac, which is why the Aquarian Age follows the current, waning Piscean Age. At first, this reverse journey through the zodiac signs was a mystery to me. Only after some research did I found an explanation.

A great deal of literature about the measurement of an astrological age mentions the Spring Equinox (northern hemisphere) or the term "the precession of the equinoxes." When the Babylonians first established the zodiacal system as we know it today, the Spring Equinox took place in the constellation of Aries. Due to subtle shifts in our planet, it takes around 2,000 years for the position of the constellations to shift to the next astrological sign. Around 2,000 years after the Babylonians made this discovery, the Age of Pisces commenced, coinciding with the birth of Christ. Very soon, the shift is due to occur again—this time to the constellation of Aquarius.

Despite this explanation offered by many astrologers, there is still a difference of opinion among students of the sky as to when the Age of Aquarius officially arrives. Some astrologers argue it's already started, and others say the age is almost here. A few assert it's still a few hundred years away, while a couple of bolder theorists have even pinpointed exact dates for its arrival.

Either way, we are on the cusp or nearly there, and we can already see the influences of the Age of the Aquarius.

A new astrological age is typically associated with a shift in mindset. In the last thirty years, for instance, we have seen an increased interest in Eastern and comparative spirituality and in holistic and naturopathic health care. Practices once considered extreme or alternative—such as vegetarianism, alternative medicine, mediation, and yoga—are now more readily accepted as mainstream interests or lifestyle choices.

To understand more about the characteristics of an astrological age, we can look to the qualities of the corresponding zodiac sign.

The Age of Aquarius

The sign of Aquarius is linked to humanitarian themes, suggesting that increased tolerance and peace is achievable. With equality as a valued characteristic, less emphasis will be placed on wealth or family name. More important will be ongoing learning and knowledge. This means knowledge will equate to personal empowerment, making lifelong learning and pursuit of information an essential success factor for the new age. With digital technology, information is now available.

Uranus, the planet of electricity, rules the sign of Aquarius. It is no surprise that we are at the beginning of an era of great innovation and electronic communication. With the sign of electricity and technology, we can look forward to more invention and intellectual achievement. Astrologers also predict a growing concern for the environment, with a continuous stream of inventions dedicated to preserving our natural resources and energy.

Evidence of the arrival of the Aquarian Age is prominent in Western countries with increased female independence through women's liberation movements and the introduction of equal pay and equal opportunity legislation. More recently, in the business world, female qualities such as empathy and cooperation have been recognized as important to organizational success.

The energies of the Aquarian Age have triggered evolution and maturation in consciousness. There is continued evidence of shifts in attitude toward spirituality. Interestingly, Nostradamus, along with his predictions of doomsday events, also forecasted a period of spiritual enlightenment after the turn of the millennium. He defined it as a period of optimism and wisdom.

Typical of this age are attitudes and practices that demonstrate increased tolerance for human diversity and sexual preferences. The concept of sex as a healthy activity, increased compassion for the environment, and the search for the divine force within are gaining popularity. This is occurring at a time when nature-based religions such as Paganism and Wicca are recorded as the fastest growing practices in the Western world. Wicca and Paganism are enjoying this growth without the need to preach or recruit converts. People are voluntarily seeking an alternative, nature-based spiritual path that is attuned to their intuitive sexuality, divinity, and connection to the natural world.

Instead of looking outside for spiritual guidance, many of us are looking within to find intuitive spiritual wisdom. We are recognizing that we have inner resources that can be enhanced with meditation and relaxation. This is consistent with a Pagan path where we want to experience and seek knowledge ourselves. With spiritual authority, we honor the divine force within us with ease and confidence.

With this in mind, we must not overlook negative Aquarian qualities of inflexibility, hesitation, and procrastination. These qualities can manifest in extreme selfishness and obsession with one's own spiritual and intellectual pursuits.

The Shift from the Age of Pisces

Currently, we are in transition from the Age of Pisces to the Age of Aquarius. We can gain a deeper understanding of the New Age by contrasting the characteristics of the Piscean Age with the Aquarian. The zodiac sign of Pisces represents duality, innocence, and some naivete. Although Pisces is a feminine sign, it is also a passive sign that sets the scene for patriarchal social, religious, and political structures. Christianity emerged at the time of the Piscean cusp and continued to grow throughout the early years of the Piscean Age. The Christians softened the harshness of a single male god advocated by the Hebrews with the introduction of Mary as a female spiritual icon, but despite Mary's presence in the age of Christianity it remained difficult for women to assert themselves in a spiritual and social context.

Aspects of the Piscean duality theme can be seen in Christianity, in concepts of good and evil, God and Satan, and saint and sinner. People became subservient to monarchs and religious leaders who centralized power and knowledge. The passive nature of this era saw less personal accountability as people surrendered personal authority to figureheads. Symbolized by two fish swimming in opposite directions, the era has witnessed great conflict. This conflict resulted in fighting between genders, cultural groups, and religious groups. Duality extended to gender imbalance, resulting in dominance of patriarchal structures. The Piscean Age is typical of an exoteric approach to spirituality where most people are supplicated to a God separate from the self.

Many astrologers define this age as one when we made many blunders for the higher purpose of learning our great lessons. The Aquarian Age is the time to enjoy the fruits of those lessons. In a continuous process of change, we learn from our past and continue to evolve. We need to ask ourselves:

What are our lessons from the Piscean Age?

How can we improve our relationship with other humans and with our planet?

Two Eras at a Glance

This table summarizes the key differences between the age we are leaving and the one we are beginning to experience.

	Piscean Age	Aquarian Age
Mantra	"I trust and follow"	"I know"
Ruling Element	Water	Air
Ruling Planet	Neptune	Uranus
Spiritual Focus	Exoteric ("god" is separate)	Esoteric (divine is within)
Religious Approach	Preach and convert	Seek own path
Gender Focus	Male dominated	Equal
Physical	Mind-body separate	Mind-body-spirit integrated
Sexuality	Sinful, repressed, celibacy advocated	Joyful, liberated, varied preferences
Power	Centralized	Democratic, self-managed
Problem Solving	Reactive	Proactive
Environmental Focus	Detached / Abuse of resources	Involved / Interest in restoration
Community Focus	Homogeneous, racist	Cross-cultural, tolerant

When we take a closer look at the comparisons we can see how the characteristics of the Aquarian Age are compatible with a Wiccan path. The climate of the New Age is receptive to equality, tolerance, and harmony. In contrast, during the Piscean Age women in particular suffered injustice and oppression. The Aquarian Age characteristics are aligned with goddess-centered spirituality, polytheist religions, and dual deity worship—all features of Pagan and Wiccan traditions.

The Challenges of the Cusp

While we are on the cusp of this New Age, many people continue to experiment, jumping from one interest to another. If we can imagine a pendulum hanging over the two ages of Pisces and Aquarius, we can see it swinging in this time of transition before it settles firmly over the point of Aquarius. For the last thirty to forty years, we have been experimenting with varied new practices while the pendulum has been adjusting to Aquarian influences. As we move into the New Age, it also appears that it takes some time to adjust. This is typical of any transition process as we adapt to the changes.

A change in mindset cannot take place quickly or overnight, but it tends to occur slowly by evolution rather than by force. Sometimes during transition, there is confusion as roles are clouded and definitions are not yet established. For example, the gay

The sign of Aquarius is linked to humanitarian themes, suggesting that increased tolerance and peace is achievable.

movement has been gaining momentum for some years now. Before it is sanctioned by society as a credible sexual preference, we must first experience the overt publicity that comes with gay marches and gay pride festivals. This is the swinging pendulum taking some time to stabilize at its new reference point.

Gender roles remain blurred as the male/female struggle continues to suggest an "us and them" mentality. In this time of unrest, as we are keen to discard patriarchy and convention, we can easily get it wrong. In the education system, many schools have shifted the focus to girls' learning needs and academic achievement. In the process, the boys have been forgotten. This has resulted in boys falling behind girls in most areas of academic performance, with lower literacy rates and higher school dropout statistics. Boys have higher incidents of teenage suicide. Researchers are quickly looking for solution to address the gap and restore balance.

The characteristics and benefits of this new astrological age will not manifest overnight, but could take a couple of hundred years to become more obvious.

What Does the Age of Aquarius Mean for Wicca?

With each new astrological age, there is a shift in values and mental models that affect how we live and how we relate to each other. A realistic assessment of our society today tells us that we have a great deal of unrest to resolve before we can comfortably say that the beauty and peace of the Aquarian Age are truly here. There is as much environmental and human turmoil as there is enlightenment. In an age of awakening and intellectual growth, we are more likely to challenge religions that impose a rigid set of beliefs and expectations.

Sitting on this cusp, we are still exploring alternative therapies and practices until we find what suits our mindset and lifestyle, and more importantly, what works for us. We are rediscovering the tools that uncover this fantastic magic that has been with us from the beginning of time. As we reach out for the ideology of a nature-based esoteric path, we also discover the infinite possibilities in our abundant world. The spiritual aspects of the Aquarian Age, in contrast to the Age of Pisces, paint a favorable picture for a religion that respects and honors a male/female balance.

The revival of goddess spirituality goes hand in hand with the growing interest in Wicca, where both women and men celebrate the dual divine force of Goddess and God. This spiritual balance acknowledges the female and male energies that form the creative life force. This is typical of the Aquarian Age that is aligned with female energies, restoring balance to the patriarchal dominance of the Piscean Age. In a time when more people are disenchanted with mainstream monotheist religion, the features of Aquarius strongly suggest that the new astrological era is Pagan- and Wiccan-friendly.

EYE OF TOAD,
EAR OF NEWT

A Wiccan/Pagan
consumer guide

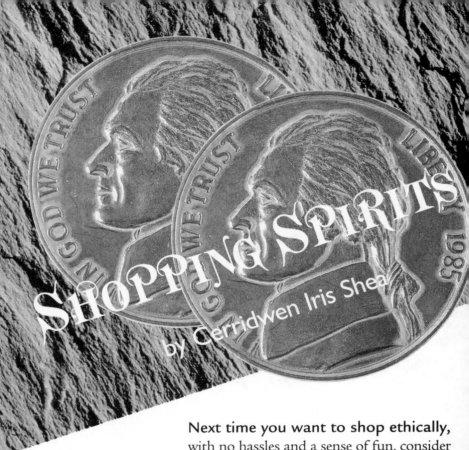

SHOPPING SPIRITS
by Cerridwen Iris Shea

Next time you want to shop ethically, with no hassles and a sense of fun, consider calling upon the shopping spirits. Before you start complaining about how it's disrespectful to solicit a deity for shopping assistance, that it's a waste of magical energy or unethical—take a breath, please.

Remember the Greeks and Romans? They endowed their gods and goddesses with characteristics and desires and, more importantly, archetypical energy. Belief and reality commingled, and the gods and goddesses became a part of everyday life. Their pantheon of gods and goddesses make present-day soap operas look positively tame. And wouldn't you know it— they had a whole bucket of deities dedicated to commerce and other such mundane tasks. If it's good enough for the Greeks and the Romans, then how bad can it be?

Besides, if you think about it, why wouldn't divine energy be interested in shopping? Didn't divine energy inspire most of the goods and services in the first place?

Taking the time to work with spirit before, during, and after shopping streamlines the process. You find what you truly need and want instead of spending money on anything that comes across your path. You're more focused. You spend wisely. You get more for your money. You're more thoughtful and plan better, and you are open to inspiration without being as influenced by advertising. You're more likely to shop at eco-friendly small businesses than at large impersonal chains. I don't know about you, but I think where I spend my money has as much of an impact as voting or serving jury duty. Part of my responsibility is to be careful where my money is spent—even if I have to go out of my way.

You can work with a variety of energies, depending upon what you want to achieve on your shopping trip. Harvest deities are a good choice—shopping is a type of harvest. Harvest spirits are especially helpful for grocery shopping. Aphrodite is great to advise you on clothes or beauty products, but she isn't always the most careful with money so it will be up to you to watch the purse strings. Generous Jupiter aids in gift shopping, but again, be careful to stick to your budget. Hestia is good for hearth and home. I also like to consult Lugh when it comes to home improvements. Since he's good at everything to which he sets his mind, he has expertise I don't have.

You don't have to work with a god or goddess, of course. If you have a household guardian spirit, I'm sure the spirit would be delighted to join the outing. I would advise leaving the dragons at home, though, unless the shopping trip is specifically dragon-oriented. I work with dragons on an almost daily basis, but since their logic is quite different from human logic I find them disruptive during shopping.

Angels are helpful. I'm not sure if there's a special category of shopping angel, but I find that my guardian angel assists when I need to locate something. I also like to invite along a spirit I called the shopping sprite—she's somewhat like a fairy, with an eye for beauty, but she's also very practical and has a great sense of humor.

How to Shop with Spirit

For a planned shopping trip, light a candle and invite along whichever spirit you wish to join you. Explain the purpose of the trip. Make a list, if possible, of what you need. Discuss budget constraints and concerns. Check the calendar. Big-ticket items can be tricky during a Mercury retrograde, yet it's a great time to attend a tag sale. Plan your route. Ask for guidance and inspiration. Remain open to the unexpected. This doesn't mean if you see a diamond necklace well out of your price range you're supposed to go in and buy it. Use common sense and discernment. Don't blame spirit for impulse shopping.

Even if you're on a tight schedule, try not to rush. The more rushed you are at the outset, the more will go wrong along the way. Instead of worrying that you won't find a parking space, believe that you *will* find a good space. Instead of shifting your weight from foot to foot and getting angry at the people in line ahead of you who aren't as fast as you want, use the time to look around and experience the store. Remember, we're living mindfully on this path. If you've experienced as much of the store as you can stand by the time you get into line, consider it a "time out." Instead of whipping out that cell phone and annoying everyone around you, practice a two-minute meditation in line. As you develop your meditation skills, you'll find you can do this with your eyes open, simply by soften-

Why wouldn't divine energy be interested in shopping? Didn't divine energy inspire most of the goods and services in the first place?

ing your focus. By the time it's your turn, you will feel refreshed and invigorated. In addition, your positive energy will improve the clerk's day.

When you enter a store, clear the doorway. It's disrespectful to enter or exit a place and stop right in the door. If you plan on being a human doorstop, at least stand to one side and hold the door for those who wish to keep moving. Wait till you enter a store to move out of the way and pause, or to walk slowly down the first aisle. Take a few beats to breathe and get the feel of the place. Let the energy guide you. I find this technique especially helpful when I enter a new store, need something specific, and have no idea where to go. While I'm searching for the directory or trying to read the signs, I'm also trying to read the store's

BRIANRASZKA.COM

energy. Often, I won't need to find the directory. I'll be able to feel out what I need and go directly to it.

Ever head for the checkout line and feel as though you've forgotten something? Get out of the line. Again, it's disrespect-ful to dump things on the counter and then run off to get "one more item, I'll be right back." It's frankly a waste of everyone's time. If you think you've forgotten something, get out of line and out of the way. Take a minute and check your list, both physically and mentally. If the feeling won't go away, breathe. Let the energy guide you to the item you forgot. Sometimes, I don't know what it is but my left (receiving) hand will start to tingle. I let my hand guide me to the item my subconscious obviously wants. And I can feel it when it's the right one.

Practice will help you differentiate between when you're being guided to something you need and when you're just in a wasteful shopping mood. You have to be honest with yourself. Sometimes we buy something on an impulse even when we know we shouldn't. Sometimes we buy something without a clue why— and then, suddenly, we realize the reason. The key is being care-ful and realistic within your budget. There's nothing wrong with buying yourself a treat or something unusual that's come along your path, but don't get into serious debt over it.

When you get your new items home, unpack them right away. Don't just dump the bag over in a corner and leave it neg-lected, where it can become a gathering point for negative or stagnant energy. Unpack it, fuss over it a bit, and introduce it to the home. Let it know it is welcome. Smudge it. Bless it. And thank spirit for joining you on the trip. Light a candle of thanks, make an offering, and add fresh flowers to your altar. Integrate yourself, the items, and spirit, and you've taken another step in a mindful, holistic life.

Live Long and Prosper

While it is important we remember our relationship to the Earth and not engage in conspicuous consumption or throwaway consumerism, it is time for Pagans to embrace abundance.

While many in our communities still distrust a materialistic society, we need to acknowledge that living abundantly, as rich Witches, doesn't necessarily result in excessive consumption. We can start by investing in this simple belief: We are worthy. And knowing this will lead to purely good things.

Let your dreams rise, and pursue them. Make the practice of abundance a regular part of your life, and see what riches come.

FINDING A GOOD HERBALIST

by Boudica

Years ago, I made my way through my college's corridors to the classroom marked "Herb Class." The school had a Woman's Day with classes on topics and issues intended to interest and attract women. This class was supposed to be a discussion by a local herbalist, but the course description was rather vague. As I wasn't aware there were any certified herbalists in my area, the whole thing intrigued me, so I scurried through the unfamiliar college corridors to her class.

I settled into my school chair and brought out my notebook. On the desk of the teacher were a few recognizable plants—echinacea, blue strawflowers, and others. I expected a lecture on the various types of herbs that grew locally, but the class that was given was much more similar to some online courses I had attended and some magazine articles I had been reading lately.

The herbalist started with an introduction to laws regarding herbalists, certification, and the practice of prescribing herbs. She gave a disclaimer regarding medicinal uses for herbs, explaining that while she was giving us folk wisdom regarding what some herbs are used for, she was not recommending these herbs for any of these uses. She also explained that she was not a doctor and could not, by law, prescribe any herb for the treatment of any kind of ailment. She said if you are ill, you should seek professional medical help.

I was dealing with a professional herbalist, and it was a delight to hear what I had already been hearing from professionals in the Pagan community for so long.

Dangers of Herbalism

I've been on so many Pagan herbal e-lists where the most common question is: "What herb can I use for such and such?" In such cases, there is always someone who will offer a home remedy without asking any kinds of questions. They are quick with the answer and never pause to think whetherthey should answer at all.

When I have questioned some of these advice-seeker regarding the speedy advice, or made a comment about laws or the possibility of allergies, the response many times has been something along the lines of "How dare you deny me my right to seek medical help from whomever I choose? If I want to use a natural means to heal myself, I will."

More often than not, these people are indignant and rude because you suggested they should take care with what they are doing. They do not want to hear that while they may have some information, they usually do not have enough.

We seek the roots of natural healing in the herbs from the earth, but the fact is many people discussing herbs on the Internet these days have little or no proper information. They have a few books referencing herbs, usually. Maybe the books are magical references, and some of them may reference Culpeper's herbal (an outdated, inaccurate, and dangerous reference book). But these sources do not give everyone an instant remedy for anything ailing them.

The fact is, a person with a little information in this area can be very dangerous.

Herbalism Tips

The first question any seeker should ask is, how can I find a professional herbalist? What criteria should I use in choosing someone to work with? You have to ask yourself why are you looking for an herbalist to begin with. Taking herbs willy-nilly is no way to go about healing what ails you.

As to what certifications an herbalist should have, it depends on your state and its laws and standards. Most states require some kind of certification to be a recognized herbalist. Always check

More often than not people are indignant and rude when you suggest they take care with what they are doing.

credentials, as these days there are many online schools with little or no background or state regulation. The school should be certified at least by the state where the school is located, and the herbalist should have certification from a state-certified school. There is also the title of master herbalist associated with someone who has gone further with their studies. Again, check the credentials.

If you check some of the schools, you won't find much standardization in the length or types of courses that make up the schools. Some offer six-month courses, others two-year courses. There are six-day "intensives" for master courses and there are ten-week master courses. It is your responsibility to research the school and the herbalist. You can find out a lot from the courses the herbalist has taken to achieve the title.

Are you are looking to study the healing properties of herbs? What are you going to do with that information? Let's look at some very serious legal issues here and then discuss what your options are.

It is federal law that you must be a board-certified doctor in order to prescribe any kind of treatment for an ailment. This law is interpreted on a state-to-state basis. Each state decides what type of certified practitioners mays prescribe. In my state of Ohio, for example, only a doctor may diagnose an ailment and prescribe treatments, including herbs and dietary supplements. Chiropractors here in Ohio are permitted to suggest dietary supplements to their patients, but that is a rare exception.

Acupuncturists, on the other hand, are not permitted to prescribe anything for their clients. The state of Ohio passed a law a few years ago allowing acupuncturists to be certified. In one well-known case an acupuncturist wrote an article for the Cleveland *Plain Dealer* about this change in the Ohio law. In this article she mentioned it was her practice to recommend Oriental herbal remedies to her clients after a session. The state of Ohio promptly notified her that she was under investigation on charges of "practicing and prescribing medicine without a license."

Laws in each state differ. You need to make yourself aware of the laws in the state you live in. Chances are, however, that you will not be able to prescribe any kind of herb unless you study to become a doctor. Any professional herbalist will tell you this right up front.

The reason for this is very clear—liability. There are numerous dangers. Consider allergies. How do you know if the person you are talking to is allergic to a particular plant? How can you test this? What do you do if a person has an allergic reaction to an herb? Can you afford a lawsuit if this person is seriously hurt by your recommendation?

What if this person is pregnant? There is a whole set of plants that are abortive in nature and are available in most health food stores. Do you know which ones have these properties? Did you know that some plant oils are also abortive in nature and should not be used by a pregnant woman? What if this person loses her baby because of your recommendation?

How long should one take an herb? Again, this is a very serious question and, again, presents liability problems for the inexperienced prescriber.

Most herbalists will tell you that any herb should not be used for more than fifteen days at a time. At that point, you should have either found relief from whatever it is you started taking the herb for, or it will not work. The best way to test this is to stop using the herb for a week. If the symptoms return, then the herb was masking the problem and should be discontinued

and better treatment sought. This is akin to when a doctor prescribes antibiotics for an ailment. The treatment lasts fifteen days at most. There is a reason for this. A certified herbalist will know the reasons and will know the dangers of various herbs and treatments.

Serious Issues

There are a few serious issues to address in our community when it comes to taking herbs for an ailment that is self-diagnosed. First of all, as you are not a doctor why are you even attempting to self-prescribe an herb? Have you seen a doctor for your ailment, and did he agree to this herbal treatment for your illness?

A good herbalist will never suggest any kind of herbal remedy for any kind of serious ailment. Their reply will rightly be: "See a doctor!" Yet we are seeing people in our community who are very sick being taken to emergency rooms because they figure a few herbs will substitute for a doctor's care. It is more costly in the long run to be taken to the emergency room of a hospital and treated for a life-threatening situation that could have been avoided, than to see a doctor first. A professional herbalist would have told you that right up front.

The other serious issue is common abuse of an herb. The one that comes to mind is the overuse of St. John's wort. This herb, available on any health food store shelf, has been suggested to treat everything from daily stress to bipolar disorder. Research suggests there may be some merit to this herb, but other research shows significant side effects to its use. The plant's properties also seem to be habit forming.

I have heard repeated comments from people who have self-prescribed the herb for themselves to the effect that they could not make it through the day without their St. John's wort. Or they just can't seem to be able to stop using it because they can not deal with being without it. While the medical profession has not yet made St. John's wort a controlled substance, this sounds like an addiction to me. Again, a professional herbalist would have applied the fifteen-day rule and suggested you consult a doctor concerning your problem if it persisted.

Other issues in self-prescribing multiple herbs are the combined effects of the herbs, or how the herbs will react with other herbs or with other prescribed medications. Again, only an experienced and certified herbalist would be aware of the true side effects of most herbs.

A woman I know was going in for major surgery in a couple weeks' time. When we were eating breakfast together one morning, she opened her purse to take some pills. Among the tablets was a capsule which resembled the many herbal capsules you buy over the counter. She then started to tell me that she had been taking ginkgo biloba for her bad memory and that this was helping her. However, ginkgo biloba is a blood thinning agent, and considering her surgery I immediately suggested she discontinue the herb and tell her doctor she was taking it. It is very clearly stated in most herbal reference books that ginkgo biloba interacts with medicines—with warfarin it causes excessive bleeding, with a thiazide diuretic it raises blood pressure, and with trazodone it can cause you to fall into a coma. Yet people pop these herbs regularly without a thought for the potential side effects and drug reactions.

Consulting a good herbalist is the only guarantee you will be safe from all the dangers.

While it's nice to be able to point out plants in the field and know what parts are used from these plants, over-the-counter herb packaging often does not tell you what part of the plant is in the tablet or capsule. While some may be obvious, some remedies, such as teas, could contain flowers, leaves, stems, or roots. You also may need to know the strength of the dosage. Various factors can greatly affect the strength of the product and consequently will affect how much a person should take.

Some other questions you might ask include: Should this be given to a child? What brands are consistent in strength and quality? How strong are the ingredients? Do the strengths vary from package lot to package lot, from manufacturer to manufacture, and from year to year?

Good herbalists will always bring these questions up and have answers that will reflect their level of expertise.

There is a lot to consider here when we discuss herbs and herbalists. There are people online, in casual classes, and in our everyday encounters that can do more damage in a few careless words than you can imagine.

As a final note, we do not even consider what we do with herbs for our own entertainment. A very common homemade item is May wine. While we may include sweet woodruff in the bottle, I have read recipes which suggest including wormwood in the mix. There is also a home-brew ale made with wormwood.

How many of us know that wormwood is a cumulative poison and we should not be using that particular item? Cumulative poisons are those that can lead to poisoning through long-term use. You build up a toxic level of this herb in your bloodstream through repeated use.

Be very careful if you are a novice or just starting out on the herbal path. Seek a professional with credentials to help you study and learn. Ideally, your sum of knowledge about herbs will not come from a book, or even a group of books. It comes from learning from professionals, doing research, talking with the person seeking advice, and knowing the law and how to adhere to it. Seek a knowledgeable person who will guide you with professionalism, wisdom, and understanding of the law.

About the Authors

Elizabeth Barrette serves as managing editor of *PanGaia* and assistant editor of *SageWoman*. Her other writing fields include speculative fiction and gender studies. She lives in central Illinois. Visit her website at: http://www.worthlink.net/~ysabet/index.html.

Chandra Moira Beal is a writer in Austin, Texas. She has written books and dozens of articles. Chandra also works as a massage therapist and reiki practitioner. Visit www.beal-net.com/laluna.

Boudica is the reviews editor and co-owner of *The Wiccan/Pagan Times* and owner of *The Zodiac Bistro*. She is a teacher both on and off the net and a guest speaker at many festivals and gatherings. A former New Yorker, she currently resides in Ohio.

Dallas Jennifer Cobb is a work-at-home mother and author in a waterfront village in eastern Ontario. She writes about what she loves: mothering, gardening, magic, and alternative economics. She enjoys the fruits of rural life: time, quiet, and a contented family.

Ellen Dugan, a.k.a. the Garden Witch, is a psychic-clairvoyant and practicing Witch of seventeen years. She is a master gardener and teaches classes on gardening and flower folklore at a local community college. She is the author of several Llewellyn books.

Emely Flak has been a practicing solitary Witch for ten years. She is a freelance writer based in Daylesford, Australia, and works as a learning and development professional. She is dedicated to embracing the ancient wisdom of Wicca for the personal empowerment of women in the competitive work environment.

Karen Glasgow-Follett has practiced witchcraft for thirty-two years. She lives in the Midwest with her husband, two sons, and a menagerie of animals. As a registered nurse, Karen teaches classes in childbirth and women's health. Karen also teaches psychic development and the arts of witchcraft.

Ruby Lavender is a practicing Witch of Romano-Celtic descent with a coven descended from Alex Sanders. She has written on herbal healing, aromatherapy, perfumery, and Pagan folklore for various publications—including Llewellyn's *Wicca* and *Herbal Almanacs*. She also teaches writing and film studies in Boston.

Paniteowl lives in the foothills of the Appalachians in northeast Pennsylvania. She was raised in an eclectic family of spiritualists. Currently, she is building a spiritual retreat center on a plot of woodland and writing a book about the Pagan community.

Diana Rajchel lives in the downtown warehouse district of Minneapolis, Minnesota. She has practiced Wicca for eight years and received a third-degree initiation in the Shadowmoon tradition in 2000. She is presently active with Twin Cities Pagan Pride.

Flame Ravenhawk teaches and writes about topics of interest to the Pagan community. Her work has appeared in many publications. She maintains a website at www.flamesfirepit.org dedicated to the exploration of shamanic Wicca and Pagan philosophy.

Steven Repko is a founding member of the Coven of Nature-Wise and an astrologer, medium, musician, and poet. He and his wife are owners of Gem N Aries in Mays Landing, New Jersey.

Cerridwen Iris Shea was an urban Witch, now a suburban Witch, and dreaming of becoming a rural Witch. She writes for numerous publications. Her website is www.cerridwenscottage.com.

Tammy Sullivan is a full-time writer and solitary Witch who works at her home in the foothills of the Great Smokey Mountains. Her first book, *Rage & the Mage,* is due to be released in the spring of 2005.

Dianne Sylvan has been a practicing Wiccan for ten years. She is author of *The Circle Within: Creating a Wiccan Spiritual Tradition* (Llewellyn, 2003). She lives in Austin, Texas. For more info, visit her website at www.dancingdownthemoon.com.

S. Tifulcrum has been a public Wiccan for more than thirteen years. Her background includes military service, clergy duties, and a variety of careers. She is happily married and the mother of a beautiful girl. Visit her at http://stifulcrum.tripod.com.